West of The Big Road

Stories of The Land & Home

Judith L. Butler

ISBN: 0615899099
ISBN 13: 9780615899091
Library of Congress Control Number: 2013919169
LCCN Imprint Name: Judith L. Butler, Palm Springs, CA

To Mama, PK, RM & The B. Gang
My Biggest Fans

WEST OF THE BIG ROAD

Stories of The Land & Home

Other Books By Judith L. Butler

THE BIG WRITE

A Journey of Words
Miss Minnie & More Forgotten Women of the West
Nevada Belle & The Forgotten Women of The West

Acknowledgement

It's hard to thank all the right people. For we are the sum of all our earthly experiences and faith journeys. There have been so many called family, friend and teacher who have enriched my life with their support and companionship and stories. I hope they all consider themselves a part of all I am today.

Thank you especially to our Mother. Whose lovely face first greeted me when I burst into this world one November day many moons ago. A fierce defender of her children who gladly gave us the best years of her life. When you have that warm cocoon to crawl out of to meet the world. Anything seems possible.

To our father PK(Philip Keough)who taught us more than he ever knew - about love of a land, the sacred power of the spirit & laughter as the magic tonic for living well- I lift up a grateful heart & rivers of love.

To my sisters, cousins & Aunts and Uncles (on the Minaberry – Hamill and Butler-Keough Branches) and the next generation bless you. You have all taught me about family and love in lessons easy and some not so easy (of loss and sickness).

For everyone who believed in me especially RM my partner and folks who came into my life quickly and left lasting footprints I am grateful. When God handed out blessings I got more than my share.

About The Author

"Judith Butler's gift is to reimagine and reinhabit lives through poetic imagery so descriptive the reader gains access to his or her own lost stories. Wind-swept dust, covering over traces of a past is gently, yet deeply swept inside to reveal a living brook murmuring beneath."

David Walker
Poet –Artist

"I have new friends after reading this book. Women of strength, character and many ahead of their time. What a debt we owe to these strong tireless creative women who have come before us. Who made our lives better and made this country better. It is a reminder of all the teachers, aunts and grandmothers next door when I was growing up."

Eleanor Ash Pyper
Writer-Artist
On "Miss Minnie & More Forgotten Women of West"

"You have that ability to paint a picture by your skillful use of words but more than that-you evoke feelings, love, sadness. Your words have a way of moving the heart."

Ruth M. Hoffman
Poet-Teacher
On "Miss Minnie & More Forgotten Women of West

Contents

Introduction

This Collection of short stories is a true labor of love. Not everyone has been given an amazing land to cherish. This gift passed down to me by my parents and the generations before them created in me a life of connectedness to place and people. A full blessing. That has made the journey rich and exciting. When I think of home it is not just one face. It is many faces of the old. The lined faces of Grandfathers and Aunties. It is the smooth soft faces of tiny babies. Those of blood thicker than water and the adopted ones. Sweet faced cherubs who belong to dear old friends and almost family. Sometimes it's not faces at all that come to mind. But rather colors and sounds. Of first light and last glow. Of summer stars and spring meadows.

Tall mountains and deep valleys. Home is never one single picture painted on your childhood mind. It is everyday voices and bright Christmas wrappings. Sunday church Bells and end of summer blues.

Home is a place so far inside you only God can see. A place sometimes so quiet you have to be the stillest flower in the garden to hear. It changes with the wearing down of time and traveler's dust. As life and death come to call and leave their mark.

Our remembrances turn the pages brown and nothing is as it was. A good thing really. For even memories must come out to the light of day and speak in a new whisper.

We must never be afraid of the journey. Of shaking off the cobwebs of the past. For beyond each tattered envelope lies a truth. That expands then one day contracts with age. Yet never ceases to fill a room with laughter and memory.

The faces of home lie within us all. We need guard them well. Home tells our stories of forgotten sorrow and tomorrows' dreams. Hold them close. Hold them tight. Promise them your heart.

Judith L. Butler

The Old Keough Town Ranch
Bishop, California

Chapter 1

A Place Called Home

It is the place that crawls beneath my skin when the question is asked and answered.

Though another place holds me now and wraps around my morning face. Says goodnight to my evening smile. I like her well enough. This new town, this fine Valley. I don't know if it will always be this way. That my new places must always position themselves in the bright light against that Sierra Valley far away. Surely another place could match those gurgling creeks and cotton clouds. Though not many could hold a candle to her majestic peaks shining with a coat of new snow. Still that is not the all of it. For home is not just about the physical elements no matter how significant they might prove to be.

Home is rather more about the scenes painted on your summer mind. The first picnic of spring, the family gathered next to a happy creek eating Mother's macaroni salad and Sunday fried chicken. The familiar Daddy laughter filling the air like a soft breeze. It was as though we did not know it then one of those treasured whispers of contentment. That would come and go with the inner and outer seasons of our lives. After awhile they blur together. The sounds, the tastes, the very air of remembrance. Until one day you cannot separate the two. You find yourself unable to see the tall sacred mountains without seeing your father coming down the walk Christmas afternoon to his little women after a hard, rugged night in the forest.

Painted images of rivers, any river will do, take you speeding across those high passes conjuring up Father's Saturday touring expeditions. How can it be that we traveled so close in miles but so far in mind and spirit? When we turned the old Ford around. Beneath the fading sky of afternoon it was as though we journeyed far and wide. It is perhaps those water color days I remember most for we left our everyday selves behind.

Tucked in the cupboard behind the cracker box. We carried our old names and floating concerns along but that was not the same. Even Mother who found it hard to leave go of the frets and worries of our ordinary lives seemed like a bird set free. Her beautiful smile lighting up the whole road. Place is not and never will be defined in geographic boundaries alone. Home is not as many have said board, brick and stone. It is the last voice of summer before we turn and go. It is the first taste of winter on the red, swollen tongue. There are some who speak ill of home and wish it to go away. How sad for them and truly impossible for how can we erase the seeds that grew into our strong branches or quiet the whispers of a morning song. Perhaps one can reinvent their own unfolding though I'm not sure how it might appear. For childhood seems to live on fine grains of magic sand. It fills the air and we breathe it in like cool water from the well. It seems when we are in the thick of it. We cannot begin to grasp a glimpse. It is only when we walk away across the lands of unbroken time. That the true essence of our gathered spirit rises up to be seen by the believing eye. So when I think of home I do not return to distant mountains. I go to a place that is holy. Within my mind. I travel through cords of memory and threads of the familiar. I walk past gardens of mother roses and the smell of pine nuts cooking on the stove. Each and All is interwoven with ribbons of wonder and mystery. Not to say that every reflection painted in the mind is flavored with light. Though it does seem time sometimes separates the chaff from the wheat all on its own. Perhaps one day this Valley that claims me now will breathe the sounds of my remembrance. Not in all ways known or imagined well but sprouting seeds planted. Not so long ago. Time will write the last chapter of the wandering spirit and so we go along mindful of the days. Hands open to the possibilities.

Philip Keough Butler "PK"
Keeping watch over his Sierra Homeland

Chapter 2

Prophet of The Pines

PK knew every back road, every crevice of those grand mountains. Had a story to tell of every stream and rolling river and lake bed from the Walker River to the once thriving settlement called Little Lake (off 395 highway). He was a humble prophet of the pines.

Weaving stories like fine woolen blankets for all who passed by. It was not required that you know him or be at all familiar with that Eastern Valley of the Grand Sierras. For PK was as generous with strangers as long held friends. To him it was rather like breathing. He must have been born with pores as big and as open as Half Dome boulders. The native Californian of pioneer and gold dust ancestry drank in the sounds and smells and seasoned tales of the mountains and her people like one savors a fine burgundy after a lavish meal.

Sadly not a single story lies tucked away or scribbled on the written page. For this WWII Soldier/butcher/army cook/father was not one to push the pen. He was more the oral historian type. A rather sad thing to contemplate. An adventuresome epic life novel unwritten. Lost to time. Imagine all those fragrant concoctions gone forever. Some threads come back in bits and pieces. When his daughters stand at the hallowed ground of their youth. Standing at the edge of the jagged ridges and craggy overlooks remnants will rise up in the mountain air.

Pieces of the PK pie will come back to them as they move about their lives in that majestic valley of those Eastern lands. Those who knew their father well would say old PK peppered up those anecdotes. More than a touch. Do not all great storytellers stir the sauce so to speak. True there was likely a blur between fact and fiction but it was a most lively blur. As has been said by many we remember the past through our own experiences. Each traveler recalls a rather different version of the same events. If this were not so the library bookshelves would stand near to empty I suppose.

This is often where a love of a land true begins. At our father or mother's knee. If this not so tall, weathered gent with the twinkling eyes and affectionate grin could care for a Land as passionately as this -that was enough for his three daughters. In time they would find their own favorite haunts amidst the tall golden cottonwoods and high desert sagebrush. In the early years the three cherubs likely adopted that special piece of earth. Simply because their father loved it so. Every day without fail he brought it to life. In his words they could see the quaking aspen by the old family cabin, smell and hear the finely robed pinon trees and ancient petroglyphs. They stood no longer as mere wood and stone. They became living breathing segments of the past. The daughters could picture the families, brown and white standing side by side gathering pine nuts for the winter when their father was a boy. They too would one day bend low beneath the hearty pines to bring home baskets full of the tasty soft pearls found beneath the dark outer shells. Their hands and clothes full of pitch and their minds intoxicated by the city of pinon trees living just up the hill from their little patch of land.

Their long rich years of growing up beneath those high and noble peaks they were one with the thunderous skies and daunting summer winds. Breathing the air of childhood. Far above the ocean floor in a land God built and sturdy men and women(some of their own blood kin)tamed. Yet never conquered as this was not meant to be. One could live side by side with the beasts of the wilderness but we were never meant to dominate the sacred lands. For it belongs to all those who live and die upon the holy ground. Their father knew this deep in his heart and mind. That he would love that Valley all his days but never come to own her. As you can never truly own the soul of another. It is held for a time in safe-keeping but in the end belongs only to God.

"Morning Deer" by Ella
Minaberry Butler

Chapter 3

The Beasts & Blessings of The Holy Ground

The couple rode along that barren stretch of winter highway in a state of traveler's limbo. Heads half full of roads left behind and space given over to the paths that lie dead ahead. There had been feasts and celebrations in the home mountains. A glad time in the circle of family.

There seemed this day of December to be a deeper quiet sitting in those high mountain passes. They did not wrap themselves in the wide arms of the forest that day as in past journeys. In winter when the walls of granite are covered with sheer ice and hard snow There is a sense of danger not seen in the other season's path.

They began to calculate the minutes until they would be over the mountain and safely towards home. They settled in for the long sojourn ahead. The woman fixated. On ads for log cabins in a country magazine when the car came to an abrupt stop.

She looked at her husband with that questioning face. He said "look over towards the road". She took off her dark glasses and could barely breathe. A haunting pair of eyes bore into the mountain air as if of painted steel. An eerie stillness came over them. Piercing all that stood between the sacred and the loud.

A lone wolf had come down from the high rock canyons. Not moving he seemed frozen in time. A sacred statue of flesh and blood in the holy peaks. The wolf's coat seemed soft as angel hair. Dusted with silver and coal. There were no words to meet this occasion and so the normally talkative duo remained in a fog of silence.

It was tempting to call out to the fiercesome beast but they knew it would break the spell. So they did not. The woman couldn't help thinking that the creature was a sign from God. Those steely eyes seemed to penetrate the eternal separation between man and beast. A haunting connection between the tamed and the wild permeated that icy chill that long afternoon on the big mountain.

For days and weeks to come the couple would think about the chance encounter and wonder at the significance of the clandestine meeting in the deep forest. The woman said aloud that she sensed it was a telling message of the need to get back to their roots. To slow down-to really see and taste the world around them. For awhile they did try to notice more. To engage themselves in the natural treasures around them. She had a deep longing to get back to being that country girl her father had raised her to be. They made a pact to spend more time in that beautiful Sierra country where she'd grown up. All because of a lone wolf 's quiet gaze in a barren canyon of deep winter.

THE LOVELY FAWNS

When I was a young girl I discovered a painting my mother had done in the back room of our adopted grandma's house. It was a beautiful deer standing in a meadow her soulful eyes looking out at you as if to remind her human family what a raw treasure these gentle creatures are in our big universe.

Tall delicate blades of green leaf draped around elegant brown country cat tails in the serene meadow in the painting. The lone deer's fur depicted in dark and light from painted shadows of a grey, stormy sky. That painting burrowed in under my skin. I see it fresh and new every time I think of these quiet gentle creatures of the forest and beyond. Being a proud member of the "Bambi" generation the elegant beasts stole my heart. It was an affection my mother and I shared. I was never able to reconcile the beautiful beasts with the hunt that ensued every fall season in our mountains. There are other species I've grown fond of and I'm pure putty for a cute pup but the young fawns are my jewels.

There were few deer down in our Sierra Valley so a sighting was always met with great excitement and pure delight. On a Sunday drive to the mountains Mother or Dad would whisper "look girls a new fawn". If possible our father would pull the car over to the side of the road for his kids to get a closer look. Many of our life lessons took place on those little trips to the back country. Lessons of taking care of the earth and respecting Mother nature and her creatures. I think father had far too soft a heart to be a hunter and none of his three daughters took it up which suited Mother just fine.

Life was not perfect growing up in the wild country. The hunting world was one of the tougher sides of the mountain paradise hard for a child's mind to understand. On a recent trip to Monterey we came across a little herd of deer in a little grove near the ocean. It always strikes me as odd to see wild creatures in tame places.

The deer had been domesticated and did not move when we passed them on the quiet road. Once the fawn's keen ears picked up the scent of a stranger her head came to full alert. Then just as natural as breathing the beauty went back to eating her tasty shrub. Later when they appeared to look through me with those soulful eyes I was drawn into their spell yet again. A stillness came over the air and we felt a longing to make the moment last. I was ten years old again sitting in the back seat of our old Ford next to my sisters stretching our bodies to see the magical specimens out the little window. Watching my parent's delight in the find was almost as delicious as the gaiety we felt. The air seemed to fill up with a fine cloud of wonder and the day took on a magical veil. Crossing paths with these lovely creatures always seemed a good omen. Of something bountiful to come.

MUSTANG COUNTRY

Horses hold an exalted place in our homeland and in our extended clan. Our Uncle Richie lived for his rodeo and small cache of horses. Our father PK loved to join in the branding afternoons at his pal Dudley's ranch and was one of the cowboys on lively cattle drives in his younger days. Cousin Andy followed in Uncle Richie's footsteps winning every medal for his riding and roping. Papa PK's baby girl nicknamed "Sundown" took to horses from the start so you might say we were horse people more or less (a few of us got bucked off more than we ever stayed in the saddle).

For years the stories of the wild mustangs drew us in and left us wishing we had a big ranch to rescue some of the old girls put out to pasture. One Saturday in May a few years back the Butler gang was headed for Tonopah to join in the Jim Butler Days festivities. As my nephew's high power truck climbed down the mountain from Montgomery Pass we spotted some wild mustangs grazing in the field near the deserted highway. They were regal and stately. We were mesmerized.

Three is a lucky number in our family. Three daughters, three grandchildren. The elegant creatures in a crooked row-three of them - took your breath away under that big open sky. We would make that same trek many years to follow- each time the mustangs would be off in the distance or near the road. When the stunning specimens would break into a full out gallop you felt as you'd stepped into a dream. Knowing they were wild, untamed and free spirits made the vision even more thrilling. In a sweet twist of fate my writer's group invited a local writer to speak on her book. It was the "mustang" woman Deanne Stillman in the flesh ("Mustang: The Saga of The Wild Horse in the American West Houghton Mifflin Company-2008"). Her book brought the forgotten herds back into the limelight- maybe their last chance for survival and preservation.

It seemed the trek had come full circle in those unexpected twists and turns of the roads West.

THE WINTER MIRACLE

She sat by the little window watching the white flakes dancing through the night sky.

Falling like soft cloud puffs to waiting branches and cool blades of winter grass. It was hard to imagine that these small pieces of ivory ice could turn the Valley into a winter wonderland. But come morning she would see they would do just that.

It had been many long winters since she had witnessed this white miracle. She felt the same wonder she had known as a child. Her nose pressed against the window then as now. Knowing the magic could fade as quickly as it had begun.

After awhile the grass began to take on a glistening coat of white. This might not be just a fleeting maiden. The ivory lady was here to stay. Her little nook grew cold as the evening wove into creeping darkness. Still she could not leave her perch. Hamill drew her jacket close trying to imagine the last time she saw such a snow falling beneath those grand Sierra mountains. It was a hazy memory. Though she remembered feeling giddy. Much as she did this night of the new millennium.

High Sierra Winter
Photo By
RM Lacy

Finally sleep got the better of her. It was near midnight when she gave in. Hamill stood by the east window and said a silent good-night to the big sky of midnight blue and dancing circles of white.

Come morning she peeked through the opening over her little bed to see what had become of the winter fest. It looked as if the whole world had been dusted with a fine covering of sparkling ice. Everywhere you looked was white and wonderous. Giant pine trees flocked with pristine clouds of pure ivory. Houses looked like Christmas cards with their rooftop covered in ribbons of snow.

Hamill's sweet town had become a Currier & Ives painting. Even the not so lovely corners seemed majestic in that winter coat. She grabbed her mother's thick jacket and headed out to survey the scene before Miss Sun came bursting out. A few lost birds were searching for food by the back fence. Caught by surprise by the early storm. Hamill saw a little squirrel scurrying towards a tall pine tree his mouth full of rations. The little creatures were in survival mode. The horses grazing in a nearby field and a few fat cows seemed unfazed by the blanket of snow covering their breakfast hay. Life as usual their blank gazes seem to say.

It felt amazing to crunch her heels into the new ice. Hamill resisted throwing a big snowball at the old barn as she admired the hastily built snowmen along the back road. Someone once said the seasons seem new and fresh each passing year because we can not truly remember their colors and scents. Now she knew what they meant. It was as if she like these little creatures was seeing it all for the first time. Hamill felt as new and alive as the deep frozen crystal quilt beneath her boots.

Hamill wrapped her arms around the open sky and breathed a sigh of deep blue gratitude. She thought about how much she had needed this little miracle that hard winter. The magical days would sit tucked away in her memory book. To remind her that the child inside was still very much in force. Like the little birds and squirrels searching for sustenance and hope. Beneath those grand Sierra peaks.

FIRST LIGHT

He went out at first light. Bundled up in a fat parka and warm sweats. While Keough was half in and out of slumberland. And back she went as soon as the front door was shut tight. Later that morning Montgomery came back lit up like a Christmas tree. Bubbling over about the amazing light-the Sierra glow. She had to smile. He's becoming one of us she thought to herself.

This long ago Virginia boy was digging in and rooting down. In Father's treasured land. PK would be happy about that. Mother, well Mother saw it coming. Her last talk with her son-in-law was about him one day crossing over the mountains and calling this Valley home. It made Keough smile that mother smile when they know their children are coming home to stay. She felt a little tug that perhaps she should have bundled herself up and gone along on his little high country adventure. No he got to be alone with those mountains –it was better this way.

He was clearly falling under the spell of this magnificent country and she best get out of the way. Let the sacred air and the deep threads of history dig under his skin as it had done for her sisters and their Papa.

And every passer through who ended up staying for a mere forty or fifty years. "I saw a beautiful deer in the meadow "he said grinning. "I got some amazing shots of first light over the White Mountains". She thought she may as well pack her bags. It was just a matter of sweet time before that Virginia boy would call this place home.

Chapter 4

Old Basquos & Strays

BASQUO PETE

On a lazy summer afternoon in the 1960's if you headed out highway 6 beneath the White Mountain Range in Mono County and took the little road west towards Benton Station you'd most likely have seen old Pete Minaberry out on the screened in front porch.

Leaning back in his old wood rocker stoking his pipe with red velvet tobacco contemplating his afternoon siesta. Chances are there would be a pot of beans brewing. On the old fashioned wood stove. Hot and ready for any unexpected traveling folks or family that might drop by hungry and dusty from the road. The smell of fresh garlic and grilled onions filling the air with primal aromas that would tempt any passer-by. Two fat wood barrels sat outside near the front porch filled to the brim with cool water for drinking. When the family came on special Sundays his grandkids would run out to fill the metal pitchers with the clear liquid for the table. It made them feel like little pioneers though they did kind of miss the television sometimes.

The old house reminded Pete of the stone maison he grew up in the old country. The old Benton place sat on a big piece of land in the curve of the road next to a sweet little meadow where you could usually find a few contented cows grazing near the little pond.

Basquo Pete Minaberry
Old Benton, California

The land behind old Pete's House was part of the Paiute Indian reservation. Where a natural hot creek ran through and pumped boiling water into some of the houses. There was no set up indoors in the way of bathroom facilities but plenty of hot water came through the old pipes to drop into the old claw foot tub and kitchen sink.

Most nights you could cut the dark blue quiet with a knife. Sitting on the front porch. Pitch black except for the soft glow of the kerosene lamps peeking through the lace curtain windows from the big front room. Rarely a car or human stirring down the deserted road. A deep contrast to the lively sounds of morning at the old place. When Pete's dog Suzi would bark at passing crows and lizards and the creek frogs would sing their little songs in the rising sunshine.

The White mountains looked more like soft rolling hills in the deeps shadows of the old Benton House. With the massive Sierra Nevada range standing tall and ominous in stark contrast at the opposite end of the big Valley.

Each day except Saturday the old Basquo began the day with the same ritual. A strong cup of black coffee sweetened up with a good dose of sugar and heavy cream, a jelly glass full of prune juice for the 'plumbing'.

A good wood fire roaring in the wood stove for both heat and to start the fixings for the noon meal. Up at the crack of dawn- sleeping in was never an option for vistors to the Minaberry ranch. Early to rise was not just a saying-it was the law of the land. There were chickens and livestock to feed and eggs to gather. Plenty of chores to finish off before lunch and the afternoon nap. The schedule might deviate if one of the Mathieu brothers stopped in from their ranch or Pete's son Richie dropped by on his way to making a delivery in one of the mountain towns.

There was a little general store a few doors down. Run by the Bramlett family who owned most of the buildings in the town including Basquo Pete's. You could find just about anything a body could need on those crowded shelves. Fishing gear, hunting paraphernalia, flannel shirts or first aid supplies. You name it and Mabel Bramlett had it somewhere in the place.

Every Saturday Basquo Pete headed the thirty plus miles to Bishop Town. To stock up on food supplies and pay a visit his daughters and grandchildren.

If old Pete was your friend he was in it for life. The long haul. He never turned away a honest man needing a meal or a few dollars. Pete was a quiet man with a little mischief in his pocket. He was greatly respected in that little community as a man of intregrity and strong principles. Honest as the day is long.

Pete spent his first season in the Sierra lands sheepherding in the high mountains. It's said the Basque made such good herders due to their nature of being able to be alone for months at a time(though a few stories are told of men who went mad without Human contact for long stretches of time).

THE MEMORY BOX

The years run quickly past wearing down our memories and change them in unexpected ways. It was some years before I rode down the long highway that leads to Old Benton Station. To the little town that time forgot. One quiet Sunday my sister GB and I packed up the camera and Sunday paper and some snacks and made the short journey back into our past. Four years younger than I am she had fewer memories of the old place. I felt a little sad about that. Yet I suppose you can't long for something you never tasted.

Perhaps I should have been happy to keep my memories tucked away. But like many of us I needed to reassure myself that time and place really did exist. That it was not a figment of my vivid imagination. After thirty years I can still conjure up visions of the little creek that ran in front of the old stone house and see the sturdy wood chicken house standing in the backyard. If I am quiet I hear the sound of the old clock that sat on the mantel for years. Chiming every half hour through days of depression, war, new birth and times of death that came to call. At that stone casa.

This is the dwelling where so many life lessons unfolded for my sisters and I. We learned about our Basque and Irish ancestry in those walls where the linoleum was cracked and weathered and the only real bathroom was an outhouse by the chicken coop.

We learned about solitude sitting on the front porch in Old Pete's straight back chairs. Some days no human sound would break the silence. We found a million and one things. To do and dream while listening to the afternoons fade into evening those summers in Old Benton. As Old Pete stoked up the wood stove to start the evening meal we were entertaining imaginary friends in the side yard. We learned about friendship watching Old Pete greet passersby with the same hospitality he accorded to long time comrades.

What was his was theirs. He made no fuss about it. It was just the way it was. There wasn't a pot of beans that couldn't be stretched to accommodate one more hungry visitor. Some of the lessons can't be measured in words. The ones about respecting nature, life and taking responsibility for others as much as yourself. The lessons perhaps hardest to learn and yet the longest to live with you.

It's funny how just looking at old black and white photographs can take you so vividly back to a time and place. The smell of garlic on the stove will also lift me up from the present time to long ago at

Old Pete's stone house. I see the worn red and white oil cloth on the big supper table and hear the dripping of the big faucet in the old kitchen. In my mind I step out the creaky back door where Old Pete kept his wire baskets to collect the eggs every morning. Out back I see the giant metal bin. Where Pete deposited his trash and where my sisters and I dug out old soup cans to play store. I walk past the tiny wood cabins where old cranky Uncle John slept when there was no room in the house before all the kids left home.

It stirs something raw inside of me to think of the years my grandfather and my Irish Grandmother Tessie spent working the land, raising children and watching the events of the world from a back row seat. No telephones or TV's. Only the transistor radio to bring news of the outside world. I remember the quiet the most. Sitting on that old front porch in the cool evening air with the sound of the crickets singing their songs. A slight breeze whistling through the tall cottonwoods near the little creek.

Our house on Brockman Lane was full of sweet noise. Reno barking, Tony Bennett crooning on the little phonograph. Sisters running through the house (when Mama wasn't looking) shouting and giggling. The quiet at the Minaberry House seemed to slow down time as well. With no sounds to break the silence you noticed things more. Grandpa cleaning and preparing his pipe, in a deep trance napping.

His big town hat over his face and the newspaper sitting open in his big lap. It was the City of normal and yet the true song of the sacred as well.

Faded Dresses

Mama found that battered old trunk
Full of summer dust and age
Near a hundred hot summers past
From the last touch & put away
Faded dresses like
Folded dreams
Lie gently sleeping as
Though it were yesterday
A woman of Irish blood named Tessie
Wore the soft coverings
Across the linoleum floor
When company came
To the old rock house
A few soft white hankies
Tucked between the wood and yellow paper
ready to dry a grand-daughter's tears

Miss Tessie's been gone most of her young
women's lives
only a picture book memory until the tender threads
from that old trunk brought her home to
them from the long ago shadows
into the light of the new century

Smiling John

In the long hot mountain summers once my sister and I were old
enough in Mama's eyes to forge out on our own our folks would
let us spend a week at old Benton-about an hour up the road from
our house. Our Basque grandfather lived in a little rock and wood
house in the quiet little village without electricity or modern conve-
niences. We loved every part of those days with our grandpa. Our

best adventure was heading out the back roads to a remote area with little signs of civilization. To Warm Springs where Old Pete's lifelong friend John Mariluch brought the sheep camp every summer up from Bakersfield. It was an exciting excursion for two country kids. It was as though we stepped on a magic carpet and landed smack dab in the open fields of Basque Country. Except for the sourdough bread (an American invention) you were immersed in everything Basque.

The food, the language, the customs. That little sheep camp was like a traveling cultural exhibit. Not a lot different for we Irish Basque kids just more concentrated. We had Grandpa Pete around a lot so we understood our heritage pretty well and had a wonderful Basque cook on duty (24/7) in Mama and Grandpa too. We were up with the chickens the day we set out for the sheep camp. Raring to go but old Pete was not one to be hurried. He would sip his strong thick coffee and ever so slowly (in a kid's eyes) savor his snails(those gooey pastries) and insist we do our chores before we headed out.

It was probably past ten by the time we filled the back of Grandpa's station wagon with the fat watermelon from town, Rosie's famous orange pie and some hard Basque cheese.

Most of the roads leading to the sheep camp at Warm Springs were unpaved so it was slow going. The scenery was pretty barren as well. Miles and miles of sagebrush and a few jack rabbits and an occasional cow rambling about in a field. It felt like hours before we pulled into the encampment. There was a little wooden camp trailer where the young Basque sheepherders came together for chow and a little vino and card playing in the evenings.

The rest of the open land was empty save for a few corrals for the sheep, a few canvas tents and the giant windmill in the middle of the little makeshift camp. Basquo Pete's compadre John would always come bounding out of the cook trailer to give us an old country welcome. To Old Pete John gave a loud greeting in Basque and then in perfect english turned his attention to my sister and I. Greeting us like long lost friends he gave us giant bear hugs and grinned from ear to ear. So truly happy he was to see us all. He had a trademark gold tooth in the front of his smile and it always sparkled in the bright sun.

John was not as tall or big as our grandpa but very strong and sturdy and muscular for a man his age. He gave off a raw energy that was contagious to those around him. The first order of business was always to show his young visitors where the soda pop and treats were kept under the big windmill. It was exciting for a kid to have full reign of their own mini mart. Then John would pour us a cup of the fresh cool water out of the windmill spout. It was by and far the best I've ever tasted hands down.

Old Pete and John would head for the cook trailer and John encouraged us to go off exploring. "Anything you girls find is all yours" he called out to us and flashed that 40 carat grin. That was all the incentive we needed to go on the hunt. We'd find French coins and all sorts of odds and ends(one search turned up a pocketknife) poking through the sage brush, tumbleweed and rocks. "Soups on" John would call out after awhile to anyone within hearing distance. Usually the young herders came back for supper but sometimes there'd be one or two around for a hearty lunch. For two adolescent girls to hang out with the dark haired handsome Basque herders was a little extra bonus to camp we didn't mind a bit. It did however make the pimply faced awkward boys back at school seem pretty lame in comparison. We kept our swoons to ourselves. Still we were old enough to appreciate a fine looking gent and engage in some innocent daydreams.

Though we had our own Basque cook in our kitchen on Brockman Lane (Mama) it was always fun to eat at the little Basque camp café. The whole place smelled of garlic and grilled onions-the smell of home to me. The hot vermicelli soup, fresh sourdough and lamb chops or steak entrée with hand-cut French fries was a feast to behold. Not fancy like a San Francisco Café but definitely 5 star on the scale of tasty.

After we'd polished off the young sheepherder's menu it was time for dessert. We soon realized Old Pete's sweet tooth was rather a cultural thing. The Basque love their sweets. Sometimes eating a bowl of jam straight without any bread to go along with it. This was perhaps the one Basque influence Mama might have not been thrilled with- for like most kids we'd rather devour a sugary candy bar than carrots any day. John's face lit up like a Christmas tree when he saw what his buddy Pete had tucked away in the cardboard box. Rosie's orange pie was a slam dunk guaranteed hit and once the creamy meringue pie was sliced up it went faster than a speeding comet.

At the sheep camp the men did all the work so we didn't even have to do the dishes (like at home). So while Old Pete and John would have a smoke and a jelly glass of dark red vino and contemplate a game of mus(card game) it was our cue to cut and run. We worked off our big supper playing with the beautiful sheep dogs and trying to communicate with the young Basquos outside the cook trailer.

We mainly smiled back and forth and tried a little sign language. They probably thought we were two silly American girls but we were under the grand illusion we were charming and semi-sophisticated goodwill Ambassadors (Ah the foolishness of youth). The only downfall of the sheep camp adventure was the old rickety outhouse that stood as the only bathroom facility. Mind you we were country kids. We'd made plenty of emergency stops along the back roads over the years but this was a bit different. The country outhouses were shall we say 'fragrant' and a bit scary to a kid(the worst fear falling into that horrid dark abyss). Add that to a sister taunting you from the sidelines and you were mighty tempted to hold it until you got back home. It was a part of roughing it that I never quite got used to. Then or now. Sometimes in the evenings the young Basque herders would serenade us(or so we thought) with a few tunes on the harmonica. It was kind of like stepping into a Sophia Loren movie my sister and I playing the cute, lovable kids.

Those summer evenings as the night air cooled and the stars spread across the big sky like butter the little cook house would fill up with laughter and the sound of Basque booming out from all corners. Watching the animated faces of the young and old Basquos joking and telling stories around the table you couldn't help smile and breathe in their merriment. Even if you had no clue as to the meaning.

It was our first taste of being outsiders in our own world. We didn't speak a word of Basque except for a few off color words that Old Pete taught us as a joke. We saw old Pete in a whole new light those magical nights and days at the Sheep camp. He was the honored elder-the center of attention. More talkative and fully alive speaking his native tongue. That was his way of connecting with his people and his homeland of Pays Basque(Basque country). For he would never in his days on earth return to his little Village in the high Pyrenees. Never see the face of his mother and father or sit at the long feasting table with his young sisters and brothers. I cannot begin to imagine how one could reconcile this sad reality. It's clear to me now how much the sheep camp visits must have meant to Old Pete torn away from his deep roots and everything familiar at age seventeen.

We lost touch with John after our grandpa died in the early 1970's at the age of 83. We heard he was living at one of the Basque hotels in Bakersfield. The old Basquo sheepman never married. I thought of him often and decided to try and track him down. He had been so good to Old Pete's girls those mountain summers. I wanted a chance to tell him how much the memories meant. I also hoped Pete's Basquo pardner could help me find the village in the old country where the Minaberrys' came from. I'd hit a wall in my searching and didn't know where to turn. John wrote a sweet reply to my note and did his best to give me some direction to my hunt.

It was within a year or so of that letter I heard our dear Basquo pal had moved on to that last herding ground. It made me feel sad and a bit old. Later when I could picture the two old Basquo pals meeting up in heaven playing mus and talking Basque it made my heart smile.

Santiago

Even the sound of the name brings to mind a strong hearty man of the mountains. Sam as folks called him came to America with his brothers from the high Pyrenees Mountains of Spain. Speaking only Basque and Spanish they became sheepherders in Bakersfield until they could earn enough money to go north to the lush open lands of the Sierra Nevadas. They dreamed of staking their own homesteads and settling in to build new families in the Land of Opportunity. They had left much behind in the old country -home and family and friends. Bravely setting out for America with little in their pockets they were determined to make it on this foreign soil.

Santiago was a strikingly handsome young Basque and in the beautiful Owens Valley he would meet a lovely young Indian woman of Paiute ancestry who would become his wife and mother to his four children. The couple would be granted a large parcel of land. For their growing family near to the heart of the Paiute Reservation.

Santiago Huarte's Son Raimundo Huarte
Looking out over the Family Land in Bishop

Santiago and his wife Elizabeth and their children worked the land hard to put food on the table and shelter over their heads. Everyone took on extra jobs to bring in money for the family. Mundo the youngest boy remembers learning to butcher at the young age of ten and working for the small grocery stores in town. Sam's greatest sorrow was losing his wife at the young age of 45. Like many of The old Basquos he would never remarry. Like Old Pete there was room for only one woman in their life.

Over the years the family raised sheep and livestock in the big open fields that would keep their families fed in the lean winters.

Once out of school and having served their country Santiago sons found good jobs with The Edison Company and the County. In small towns where there aren't many opportunities for steady employment so this was a true blessing.

The Huarte daughters were beautiful like their mother. Pauline went on to win the Rodeo Queen Contest at the Town's big Homecoming week-end one year. The Huarte girls worked hard in school making their parents' proud. Pauline and Jeanette worked in the Bishop schools and the Town hospital over the years. All of Santiago and Elizabeth's children stayed on that fertile soil where they raised their own children.

Today some of the great-grandchildren have become the fourth generation to grow up on this strong parcel of Land their ancestors settled long ago beneath the shadow of Mt. Tom.

The Owens Valley like the rest of America went through the hard times of a World War, A fierce battle for water with Los Angeles and the deep depression. The Paiute leaders would begin building schools and clinics and more businesses within the reservation to build more jobs for their community. Much would change over the years as the seasons passed and Santiago grew old. Born in the 19th century the old Basquo would live to see a new era and more babies in the Huarte clan. Today Santiago's children and their children 's children still hold the land of their ancestors and have worked to build the Town of Bishop and the reservation strong. A legacy once seeded by a brave young boy who traveled from the high mountains of Spain to find his destiny in the hills and granite peaks of the Sierra Nevadas.

Strays

Rarely do you see an old Basquo riding around the back country without his sheep dog beside him in his worn in pick up truck. Chief Mundo (a Basquo & Paiute leader) has buried more old pooches in his backyard than most people have relatives. Wooly haired and some with piercing eyes they are his pals, sidekicks and his good talking buddies.

His partner LW took in strays of all varieties. Chickens, lambs and even a couple of rescue burros. When they'd get a few new lambs LW would name them. One time she gave them Beatle titles-"Ringo -Paul – George". Later she decided that made it a little harder come butchering time. The burros safe from the chopping block she named Willie & Waylon for her country favorites. The Huarte animals had nicer digs than most country animals and a few people. Sharp little wooden dog houses and sheds and wire pens. The Barlow Lane beasts had a good thing going.

There comes a time in one's life when you need a good listener and dogs are surely brilliant at that. Though they sometimes fall asleep just when you're waxing poetic with your best stuff. They make up for it in other ways.

Our father had a pal who lived at the little Meadow Farms apartments off Highway 395. We liked to tag along on his jaunts and one day we pulled up to hear his buddy yelling out from the front stoop "Dammit come here". We began giggling and Papa said with a fat smile. "Hey kiddos that's the dog's name but don't go getting any ideas now". That story's lasted for many moons and still brings a smile. Most country folks had large breed dogs whether they were mutts or of the more pure variety. Good for herding sheep, a few head of cattle or keeping watch over the ranch. You could spot a city folk a mile away with their little pampered pooches. Most of the country dogs didn't get much time in the houses. They stayed outside in the elements or come winter on back porches or wood sheds.

The most favored breeds seemed to be black labs, Australian shepards and collie mixes.

To this day the sound of barking dogs makes me feel safe and in distance of home. Back I go to Brockman Lane the sweet harmony of old dogs calling out to the world that somebody was coming down the lane for a visit or bearing bad news.

Many of the folks who had no pups in their life seemed a bit lonely. We three girls couldn't imagine our world without our animals. A couple of swell dogs (Reno, Spot & Ginger to name a few) , an ornery buck in the back pen and a sweet lamb or two.

They were such a part of our lives. Taught us a lot about trust, responsibility and friendship. If a love of animals is a gene that gets passed down it surely got handed down to our generation and the one below. It seems in every photograph-formal or otherwise- of Belle and Jim Butler there's a little furry pup or full grown pooch right smack dab in the center of things. Next to Old Jim and his model A jitneys or ready to jump in a horse buggy. In the back forty with Belle Butler at the Big Pine Ranch in her rumpled working clothes. I hear from cousin Helen that my father's mother Edna had a firm dislike of cats as they were inclined to go after her precious birds. We definitely lean more towards being dog people. Except for a few stray felines that somehow got adopted into the clan. PK's grandchildren have carried on the family tradition in providing dandy homes and buckets of affection to their sweet pooches: Ellie, Crystal and Toby. Not bad locations either. Toby has his own gigantic grassy back yard with a Sierra creek running through and his cousin Ellie and little Crystal both have nice beach houses for barking, sleeping and looking for love on their neighborhood jaunts.

It seems no matter how long your lease runs on this earth you never forget your childhood pooches or other beloved furry critters. The only hard part of this relationship is letting them go when their time runs out. Though I have it on good authority(Miss Marian-dog whisperer & canine defender) that there's a dog and pet heaven for our four legged family members. It's comforting to think they may be waiting for us on the other side.

The Ancient Bristlecones
Photo by
Gordon Rosno

Chapter 5

Land of the Sacred

The Sierra mountains have always stirred something up in me. As you drive due north on 395 from the little town of Bishop the high stone monuments seem close enough to touch. The strong sun rays beam off the granite crevices like new diamonds. On a Sunday drive near the small Village of Mammoth Lakes we turn down a remote road in search of the lush green meadow our father visited when we were young.

Some forty years later I can still see the blades of grass blowing gently in the afternoon breeze inviting the child inside us to run free across the soft blanket. Barefoot and gleeful.

In the middle of the meadow my father's old pal Dave Jackson took up temporary residence in a little rickety wood cabin for the summer.

Old Dave was always glad to see his buddy when he recognized the unexpected visitors coming down the road. A big grin would spread across his dark worn face. Usually father would come calling with a little treat in the form of fine meats(fresh jerky) or sweets. That made the grin wider and last even longer. Old Dave seemed ancient to my sisters and I but he had a young spirit. He seemed to delight in everything around him.

His dark eyes twinkling and his contagious laughter. There should be a special word for people with old souls and young hearts. It would've fit Dave to a tee. The little cabin was very rustic but to a child it seemed like a painted dream.

To live out in nature in a wide open meadow under the big mountains. Enough grub to last you for months and nice cool breezes in the full tilt of summer. I fantasized of our whole family joining the cabin dwellers for the long hot months.

My father likely would have been on board as well had it not been for that thing called a j-o-b. He almost never turned down a mad adventure.

Old Dave didn't seem to have much in this world. At least when it came to material goods. Yet he seemed like one of the most contented souls I ever knew. Even after he lost his sight there was a calmness about him. Old Paiute Dave was as much a part of that Sierra land as the tall cottonwoods and gurgling mountain creeks.

When summer was over Dave could be found back on the Bishop Indian reservation in his little house down the old country lane. He worked leather hides to make quirts and working gear for ranchers and cowboys. Father would stop in to visit and show me Dave's amazing handiwork made even more surprising considering he was nearly blind. When I drive through open country in little towns I've not met before I think of all the lives lived out in sweet houses and old cabins. Of vast generations who have called the The land their own through all the changing seasons of their life. It seems to me few folks have that same bond with high rises and concrete boxes. Those who have never really come to love a land as their own are missing something important. But it's never too late to find your own tall mountain or sweet town to claim.

MISS MAY & THE YELLOW HOUSE

The old Indian woman sat on the stone wall at the Bishop Town Indian museum As if she was waiting for a fine city photographer to take her picture. Her pure white hair thick as new grass was tucked under a big floppy sun hat. She wore a loose fitting flower dress that fell down around her curves like a soft blanket. Something drew me to her. Her beautiful brown face was like a finely etched road map. It was a strong face.

Neither shiny or new but reflecting a soft light of stories meant to tell. There was a drummer dancing in the front of the little stone museum. I drew up close to the low wall wondering if she would see me as an intruder or friend. Miss May as she called herself smiled in my direction. As though we had met at another place and time. I later wondered if she might have known my grandmother Tessie from Mono County.

Or my great Aunt Vada or my father. Though I could have imagined some deep connection it might have just been she was friendly to all younger folks who showed interest in her stories. "I live down the road in the little yellow house" she said proudly and invited me to stop in. (a dose of pure small town hospitality). The sun was warm on our faces. I longed for some cool water but didn't want to break the spell.

Miss May began to talk of the time she and her people were moved from their land up north and given names by the local white families. Uprooted from their native soil. I felt my face growing flush. I wondered if my ancestors were a part of this. I looked for recrimination in her face but there was none. I had known there were deep tears shed. In those high mountains and long winter rivers. Battles fought and wounded on both sides. It had come to seem far away from my generation. Ancient history. But sitting before this sweet woman who shared my grandparents and great-grandparent's homeland it suddenly took on a truth pretty hard to shake.

That fall day of Indian summer it became hauntingly real. To this grand-daughter of pioneers and Basque Irish immigrants it brought back stories of my grandmother being out on her own at age twelve. Her mother lost in childbirth, her father murdered for his land.

For a moment I wasn't sure my new friend knew who I was. Perhaps she was reliving her family's sorrows. So vivid in her mind. Retreating to the long ago. Of leaving their homeland. That dance of memory re-visited in all its power and force.

I'd intended to go down the road to see my own mother who would be in her little garden. Tending her roses. But once again I could not break the spell. Could not walk away from her stories and the chance to set the history straight.

I knew I would stand near and listen as long as she found the words to tell of her long journey. When she was out of stories and looking out over the cottonwood trees turning colors across the big highway I knew it was time to go. Miss May smiled at me and told me again where she lived down the next lane.

She was eighty some years old and had outlived all my ancestors and some of her own. She worried out loud that the young Indians didn't care enough about the old ways. That the traditional native crafts would be lost. I carried the memory of that day with me for a long time. Of her rough hands and kind face. I knew she would likely not remember my words but it was enough that we had shared our sorrows and laughed at the craziness of the world. Beneath God's open sky two generations of the sacred lands found a way to touch hands across the high Sierra mountains.

I was leaving town a few days later and would not be back for a handful of seasons. Many months later I drove by the little yellow house that seemed quiet and empty. I wondered if May was still of this world. I longed to knock on her door and say hello but knew deep down knew she would not recall our meeting. It seemed I should leave the new memory of our sweet time together as they were imprinted on my thirsty mind.

A QUIET MAN

He was a quiet man. One of those men of that previous generation who sit awhile in a room before anyone notices them. He did not have the need to call a lot of attention to himself like many do. Mr. B. always seemed just happy to be there. Perhaps lost in his own thoughts and ponderings. With a ready smile and genuine concern for others. He was one of those truly honest guys. What most folks call a good man. A devoted father and grandfather. The kind of attentive husband most women would love to have by their side. He put family first. Worked his fingers to the bone to provide a good living for his family. That doesn't mean he was perfect. He'd be the first to say he had a few flaws. He was salt of the earth and had definite opinions about things and would tell you about them in his own respectful way.

In all the things that mattered he was aces. His other passions were hunting and fishing and building things. When the family was living in southern California he would bring his sons up into the backcountry of the Sierras passing his love of the outdoors onto the next generation. They spent days eating out of cans, sleeping in the wild engaged in the hunt for winter meat. Memories that his sons decades later still hold dear. There were a lot of lessons about life in those woods. Down those country roads.

Mr. B. was a handsome man, even when Father time etched lines across his tanned face and the body slowed down a bit.

Still he could work circles around most folks even with his engines cooling with the badge of age. He spent a lot of years and his sons' growing up -in the big city. As soon as he was able he packed up the family's belongings and with his wife of near to 40 years headed for that same open country he'd come to love on those summer pack trips.

The couple found a perfect little house(the sons were grown & gone by then) near a country creek with a big yard and a fine little workroom for all his assorted projects. The town Big Pine, was named for the giant pine tree at the edge of town. The awesome Sierra Nevada Range sat on the west side of the little house with the rolling hills of the White mountains off to the east. It was a quiet piece of paradise. There were just a few country café's and gas stations. A few motels, school and a library. Not much else and that suited him just fine.

Finally he had the chance to do those things in life you tend to put on the back shelf. For months and years. He was given the most precious gift of all. Time.

He built a beautiful wooden playhouse cabin for his young grandson, helped his sons and neighbors mend fences and signed up for the volunteer fire department. No matter what new roads life would take him on - his spirit would remain firmly planted in that little valley. His own little slice of Sierra Heaven.

Veteran Horseman Lester Cline & A Fellow Cowboy
Carry The Flags at the Local Bishop
Homecoming Rodeo

Chapter 6

Dusty Cowboys & Colorful Characters

❧

RODEO MAN

He'd been broke more places than he could recall. Sewed together-bandaged up. Almost as good as new. If you don't count morning getting up. And winter's stiffening. The docs told him "you're too old to ride". To hang up the dusty reins & lasso's. May as well stop breathing he thought if I can't saddle up –I'm done. So he dusted off shoulders back as far as they could go - boots pointed north. He rode that bull -would show them all. Landed hard. Spit out the fresh dirt. Squared his torso as best he could. Old Les & the pick-up gals saved his skin. He strode past the rangy lot. A lil bent & broken yes. He looked 'em dead in the eye & knew this rodeo man was through- he'd made his last hurrah the only thing left that wasn't broken up was aching beyond any horse hurt he'd ever known.

Like The Wind

He was lean. Like a young cottonwood not fully rooted in. He was just as home on a saddle as any two legged creature I'd come across. When that magnificent horse broke into a deep gallop you could almost hear country music dancing in the afternoon breeze.

Watching the horse and rider glide across the big arena was something to behold.

No treasured piece of art in any fancy museum had anything over this vision of grace. I was young then. Too green to understand much of what life had to offer. Still we knew there was something sacred in the act of human and beast coming together beneath the Sierra clouds. Lester was a dear friend of our father. A very quiet man. Which I suppose made the scene more memorable. It was clear to us where Lester found his true voice. High atop a fine horse moving in tandem with the morning air as if they were one. There was no need for fancy words. No need for long winded introductions. If you had eyes you just knew.

That you were seeing something holy. I was always a little afraid of the lovely four legged creatures as a child. Most especially when you are standing within a few feet of them. They seem so massive-so powerful.

Dangerous even. We had seen more than one rider brought to his knees and bound for the hospital by this magnificent breed.

As he grew older Lester's hair turned silver grey and his straightaway gentleman's gait slowed down a bit. Yet when that cowboy climbed on his favorite cutting horse he was near twenty again. Smooth and even. Strong as a winter oak in full command. Age didn't matter so much when you were riding high upon these master beasts. It only seemed to weigh in if you found yourself dusting off your traveling blue jeans in the soft Sierra soil. Your lungs fighting for air and your bones as brittle as new ice. Then the years that piled up like silver dollars mattered. Mattered big. As long as you kept your boots in the saddle and fought gravity for the fierce competitor she was you were fine.

It's good to think there are still places where age is not paramount. Places where the worn in song of experience brings something more to the table rather than taking it away. We never thought of Lester as old. Seasoned maybe, worn in like a fine pair of leather boots but never old. We watch the young ones now. Full of fire and show. Can't help but wonder if they will ever come to glide in a saddle like Mr. Lester. It seems doubtful as the mother stream running backwards. He was one of a kind that cowboy. One of a breed. That doesn't come along everyday.

He's gone now like so many of his breed. They retired his big cowboy hat to the town's Indian museum. Every time I see it hanging there I imagine Lester might be nearby. Getting his favorite boy ready for a ride out into the afternoon sky. With more grace than a falcon.

I may have been young those hot summers of long ago as I memorized the look of Cowboy Lester gliding on those big dancing dreams but I was old enough. To know I was witnessing a grand vision. A rare gift. The rodeo arena will always seem a little too empty without Lester and his beautiful colts. It seems that we will have to remember that once there was a man who rode like the wind.

Cowboy Conway

Richie Conway by all accounts was a small cowboy even with his boots on but what he lacked in stature he made up for in spirit and a dynamite personality. The old fellow had a life force that was unequalled in those big Sierra mountains where his family settled back in the Mono Basin in the early 1900's. Richie and his wife lived in the Benton Valley for many years "sheeping". Tending the flocks, taking the herds through the little town main streets in the early days. Shearing the sheep by hand and later getting the animals ready for market.

Old Conway had a laugh the size of Texas. You could hear that deep raucous laughter. For miles and towns away. Richie was a longtime pal of our Papa's, grandfather and Uncle Richie's (likely named after the old cowboy). Richie Conway was like one of the family. Along with his sweet, soft-spoken wife Tweed. They seemed to balance each other out. Her calm to his full zesty life force. The Conways were everybody's favorite couple. They were like salt and pepper or ham and eggs. You couldn't quite imagine one without the other. Both rock hard workers even in their twilight years.

Their hard sadness in life was losing their son John Conway in WWII leaving just one other boy Adrien. Richie might be near the same size as some of the fat hay bales he threw off his old pickup truck but that didn't slow the cowboy down one bit. He might've been a little bent and twisted up but he was going out with a big round of salty jokes and his boots on. Richie outlived a lot of his hard living, hard riding cowboy buddies and was called on again and again to stand up for his pals at the local funeral parlor. Often in his blue jeans and dusted off Sunday boots he became a solid fixture at many a funeral procession.

It seemed odd to see our laughing fellow looking so solemn and quiet but as soon as the smoke cleared the old cowpoke would be grinning. Offering up a spirited tale on the poor bloke headed for that big rodeo in the sky. In a quick country minute he turned the tears into deep red smiles.

Richie loved everyone and everything on the planet. Dogs, kids, old folks(and in between) and especially his herd. The assorted cows and horses he kept around the old Ranch likely got their snoots full (they say he could talk the ear off an elephant) and a heaping dose of that sweet cowboy affection he doled out so generously.

Folks came and went at that last Conway Ranch that sat on the corner of 395 and Brockman Lane near the little Brockman Country Store and gas station.

Richie was always good for two bits for any curious kid he came across in town or on the street. His hip pockets were full of more stories than horse manure at a rodeo. Once he got rolling –spinning his yarns no one dare leave the corral or café until he brought the punch line home. You didn't want to miss a second of his lively tales. And you could be sure that the salty chronicle would be circulating by nightfall at McMurry's and Rusty's Saloon. Old Richie Conway was our own Will Rogers and Mark Twain rolled into one sweet and savory cowpoke.

My own personal favorite story was one Basquo Pete Minaberry told on his longtime Pal. Pete and Tessie's fourth child was about to be born at Benton Station around 1930 in the dead of winter at the old rock house the family rented from the Bramlett Family(for $40. a month). Tessie was not a young woman-over 40 years old and Big Pete wanted a doctor on hand just to be safe. He sent Cowboy Richie to fetch the doctor As the nearest hospital was near to 40 miles away. The labor wore on and there was no sign of Richie or the country doctor. Pete told his grandchildren and Basquo pals "Old Pete take care of Mama. Pretty soon the baby ready to come and no doctor. No Richie. Baby no want to wait for doctor so Papa Pete help the little guy come out. Clean up the baby boy and the Mama. Put the baby in the blanket and put him next to his Mama.

Here comes Richie with doctor. He says 'good job Pete-that'll be sixty Bucks." It Turned out Richie had stopped off at the Yellowjacket Mine and got sidetracked with a little libation and delayed retrieving the 'doc'. Thankfully all turned out well in the end.

It seems like the whole town's a little too quiet since that old Cowpoke left us some years back. They moved his old ranch house to Laws outside of Bishop Town. On 395 there's no trace of the place he and Tweed called home for many years. Where so much old west history played out. Where water wars were fought, soldiers sent off to war and the cowboys and Indians(Paiute mostly) lived side by side. Raising horses and children and decades of living lean. Of welcoming new folks to the beautiful Valley. As well as too many sad goodbyes to old timers and friends beneath those grand Sierra mountains West of the big road.

Charlie Keough-Mining Man

At our old two story house on Brockman Lane in Bishop we loved to see company arriving outside the front gate. There were a lot of interesting folks that stopped in at that old half acre homestead that was situated in the shadow of Mt. Tom.

When one of us would spot the funny little blue jitney we knew Charlie Keough was making his rounds to call on pals and assorted relatives. Charlie was a tall distinguished gentleman that reminded us of a spiffed up version of Grandpa McCoy on tv. He seemed very old to us because of his voice that kind of cracked, his thin skin and stark white thinning hair but he might have just been in his sixties. He didn't resemble any of father's other buddies in his dress or speech or mannerisms. He was a rancher and a mining man but more on the management side I would guess. No matter how hot a Sierra day it might be old Charlie would come up the stone walk in a freshly pressed white shirt, a fancy department store tie and fine brand trousers. It didn't stop there. Charlie would be sporting some high quality dress shoes that looked like the cow may have put up a fight (they looked so new). We were more jc penneys and hand me down folks but we knew expensive when we got close enough.

Charlie always arrived from his Peavine Ranch in Nevada with a fat suitcase full of colorful stories. Hearing papa's cousin (once removed) spin a yarn was like going to a big lecture hall to hear a great orator. Father would offer Charlie some libation and as

I recall he rarely took anything stronger than iced tea then the tales would fly. Papa would usually let us hang out in the big living room feeling that this was the best education a kid could have of the history of the old west (he was so right). Since Charlie had a soft voice we'd lean in so as not to miss a word. For hours Charlie would weave tales of long lost relatives, mining dramas and report on who died or landed in a heap of trouble. It never seemed mean or petty like gossip. He was more like a traveling Walter Chronkite. That old duffer as papa used to say was a genuine storyteller much in the caliber of Will Rogers or Mark Twain.

In my memory it seemed Charlie rarely stayed for supper. He had a long list of folks to see on his road trip jaunt around the Owens Valley and beyond. Often his end destination was to land in Los Angeles where his sister Inez resided with her husband Albert and a cat or two. They grew up in the mining town of Austin but took far different roads out. Inez loved all the culture and festivities of a big city. Whereas Charlie after garnering a degree in engineering at a prestigious school(Stanford as I recall)headed right back to his desert roots.

He seemed far more comfortable with country folks than the highbrow city lads. With his beautiful and gentle bride Marian they called the Peavine Ranch home for many years.

After losing his dear Marian old Charlie continued to serve as the perfect host to wandering prospectors and assorted shirt tail relatives who dropped in at the property in rural Nevada. Filling their stomachs with good eats, country libation and a pocketful of lively tales.

When you stepped into the ranch house past the beautiful yellow roses on the front path it was another world from the open lands and rural landscape. The picture of elegance awaited visitors within those four walls.

Fancy velvet chairs and settees and elegant mirrors and hand carved wood bureaus. We girls were a little afraid our worn in blue jeans might dust up the fine furniture but Charlie didn't seem to worry about such things.

When we got word Charlie had passed away the whole Keough Clan made plans to attend the funeral in Austin an old mining town in Nevada. An assorted bunch of cousins and I rode in the car with Auntie Laura and cousin Cindy. We all stopped in Tonopah for some grub at the Mizpah. Cafes were few and far between on that barren stretch of open road. Our little caravan stopped somewhere outside Tonopah for gasoline and a very old gent with whiskers and red eyes asked us "where all you folks off to in these parts"? When Auntie Laura replied we were headed to Uncle Charlie's funeral the old fellow let out a yelp and a big grin "yeah they'll be coming from hell to breakfast to say good-by to old Charlie". That scene has stuck with me for nearly forty years.

The Keough Clan gathered at an old country saloon to warm up and for the adults to toast Charlie in proper country style. Charlie's only sister Inez was a vision in that dusty bar with her dark dress suit ensemble, a chic hat and a fox stole(the fox heads looked none too happy) Though she was not a big fan of the drink she was a good soul. To have the day be what old Charlie would have liked. It was my first burying in deep snow-the folks shivered a little but we all stayed to the end of the minister's words.

I don't remember much the preacher said that day but I knew it was a special time. All his kinfolk had come from near and far to pay their respects to their dear Uncle, cousin and brother. A sacred thread tied us all together young and old and in between. A testament to loyalty, duty and love. Our ancestors' blood and bones were shed and buried in those Nevada hills, back roads and worn down cabins. Family sticking together in bad times and good. We may all roam far and wide from these parcels of earth that hold our deepest roots. Still we will always know who we are as people and where we come from. In my book that says it all.

The Elegant Mrs. Hugh(Marjorie) Brown~
Author of "Boomtown Lady"

Chapter 7

Boom Town Lady &
Tonopah Town

There was this little book on Auntie Elma's shelf in Hollister Town that also was part of my Aunt Belle's and cousin Inez Keough Herman's library collections.

The family women urged me to read the colorful memoir. Said if I wanted to get the true flavor of the old West mining days from a woman's perspective this was the book. "Lady in Boomtown" turned out to be a candid peek inside Mrs Hugh Brown's twenty years of rugged living in a western Nevada mining camp (Tonopah). Having grown up in the gem of the West- San Francisco Mrs. Brown found the wild and wooly mining camp a bit of a shock. Reading this tale of a woman of culture, a graduate of prestigious Mills College surviving desert housekeeping, political scandals and a town fixated on the world of mining. I felt like I'd stepped smack dab back into 1900. When Aunt Belle announced that Mrs. Brown was still living-residing in a retirement home in San Francisco. I wasted no time in tracking down the name of the place and made arrangements through her daughter Jerrie to meet up with the two women the following week.

I wasn't sure what to expect by meeting with this remarkable woman so tied to the threads of my family's gold dust heritage. I imagined Mrs. Brown had crossed paths with my great -grandmother and other members of the Butler Clan. Deep into the big hunt of the pages of the past to finish my own book on the Women of the West I couldn't wait to meet the author- trailblazer.

The address of the place led us to the Marina at the edge of the Bay. A beautiful spot and an impressive brick building. Unlike any retirement home this country girl had ever seen.

We later learned the amazing structure was built by Julia Morgan - a famous architect of that era. Inside the stately halls everything was spit polished and sparkling. Mrs. Brown's room sat at the back side of the building so there was ample time to get a few butterflies. I hadn't written out a lot of questions not wanting to overwhelm the elderly author in our first meeting.

Mrs Brown looked very regal and dignified as I entered the little room and greeted her daughter. Her hair was done up in a lovely upsweep and she wore a stylish silky patterned dress. She was the picture of elegance and I was touched she had taken such care for our visit. I could not tell her age but guessed her to be in her late eighties as her days as a young bride in the old mining town (Tonopah) went back to the early 1900's.

There was a little awkwardness initially and I grew a bit hesitant to launch into twenty questions. We exchanged small talk for a bit then spoke of her Book and the early mining days in Nevada. It was clear she didn't remember much of the history from that time. It was after all long ago and far away from the edge of the Bay.

Later I learned Mrs. (Marjorie) Brown drew from her diary notes from 1904 to 1922 to write her autobiographical tale. Therefore it wasn't required that she remember every fragrant detail of her colorful western venture.

My strongest memory of the afternoon came when Mrs. Brown said in a quiet voice "I always wondered what the Butler family thought of my little Book?". It hit me then.

That this visit was not just about my search for finding those lost pieces of the past. The elegant woman sitting before me had led an adventurous life in the desert lands of Nevada (Tonopah town) as a young bride and coming of age in the magical City by the Bay in her golden era. This was a chance for the first time author to find closure on an important Chapter of her life. I choose my words carefully. Feeling as though I'd been deemed the family spokesperson. I told Mrs. Brown the women in our family who'd read "Lady in Boomtown" enjoyed her tales of life in the rough and ready mining camp and delighted in her attempts to bring some level of decorum to the primitive conditions. Her tinted glasses hid her eyes somewhat but I could see a sparkle and her smile grew warm. That said it all. The beautiful young woman looking out from the slightly worn Book jacket- remained still a Lady of grace and timeless beauty.

I came across some old clippings my Aunt had tucked away in Mrs. Brown's Book.

In 1968 when the Boomtown Book was published(American West Publishers –Palo Alto) Mrs. Brown's memoir was big news. In a faded article from the San Francisco Chronicle she offered "I was a high powered girl. We were a different kind of pioneer. If I had to do it all over again I would plunge in without hesitation". Later in her life she would engage in dramatic readings and offer her talents to various San Francisco organizations and charity events.

A Sign of The Times~ Belle & Jim Butler Ranch (mispelled)~
In Monitor Valley, Nevada

It turned out the "Boomtown Lady" would not be long for this world. It was my last chance to cross the boundaries of time and place and step into the breathing halls of history. A good day in the vast journey that began with my father's first lessons of the past at our town cemetery and a poet daughter's long search for her deep and winding roots.

BACK AT THE RANCH

My sisters and I grew up knee deep in ancestral dust from a very early age. Our papa delighted in the stories of the big Butler silver strike and he would bring out the trunks full of photographs and letters and old mining stock papers at the least provocation.

Though we lost our family historian far too soon many of his treasured keepsakes have remained behind. After hearing about the Butler Ranch for years we decided to go on the hunt. We had no memory of papa taking us out to the remote Monitor valley place where the Butlers lived a rather simple, meager life. Living off the land like a lot of folks back in that day raising vegetable and livestock to feed their family. We passed Tonopah and headed in the direction of Belmont where our great grandmother Annie Luce was buried. We took a little unexpected detour then got on the right track. It was a rather barren road. A lone house dotted here and there. Few and far between. It began to register why some of the Tonopah folks were adamant we should tell someone where we were headed when we took off. We thought "hey we're country girls"-PK's daughters. We weren't worried But maybe we should have been. When we finally got within a few miles of the place we knew PK was smiling. We were surprised to see a road sign listing the Butler Ranch in bold letters. The only thing they had misspelled the name and it read Bulter instead. PK would have got a giggle out of that. It wouldn't be the first time our name took a hit. We've had our share of Butter and Buttler spellings. The sign made me think of finding Old Jim's new tombstone at Old Sacramento City Cemetary a few years back.

Volunteers had generously raised money for the stone and joined with our cousin Jim Whitacre efforts to have a proper memorial for the old Prospector. It's a beautiful stone with an impressive engraving and an image of Jim and his famous burro but as fate would have it the unmarked grave was right next to the latrines(built long after Jim died). That would have made our eccentric great-grandfather smile(he'd originally requested to be buried sitting up in a chair) and would have gotten a giggle out of PK too.

Back to the Ranch story. Sister Sundown maneuvered her SUV down the rocky dirt road And we talked of how impossible it would've been to ride a buggy over this rough terrain. Up ahead at the end of the road was a beautiful green meadow and down another dirt path were some old broken buildings. I got goose bumps thinking this was the place that Belle Butler wrote about in her diary. Long days of baling hay, of nursing sick cows and saying good-by to dear family pooches. This was the humble beginnings of a family who would go on to make old west history with their strike in the area the Indians called Tonopah-meaning 'little springs'. No one seemed to be around but there were signs of life about the place. There was a little creek up near the old structures and I recognized the little rock house from an old photograph of my grandfather Frank likely taken in the 1930's or early 1940's.

As kids we'd driven down every back road of the west with our father but we had no memory of this place. All those years I'd pictured the Ranch in a desert area rather than a lush green paradise. I could not have imagined how remote the place was though there were a few neighboring ranches down the road. You would have no choice but to live off the land living this far out from civilization. The winters likely were brutal backed up against the mountains at that altitude.

This was definitely not a land for the weak of body or sickly. If you didn't have grit going in you darn well had it leaving.

We wondered who owned the property now but never saw any sign of anyone. It was amazing to think nearly 130 years ago this was the start of our family history. After some time by the meadow we jumped in the car and headed back in the direction of Belmont town. It was a great ending to a fine day of discoveries. We stopped in at the cemetery to leave some flowers for Belle Butler's mother Annie Luce who came over from the Isle of Man. Then in typical Butler style we headed for the gathering place-the Old saloon down the hill from the graveyard. The fellows in the place bought PK's girls a beer and told a few stories of their own. One of Minnie Perchetti's boys(an old Nevada family) pointed off to a wooden structure and told us it was one of Jim's outhouses.

We all had a good laugh. PK would say "if you gotta go you gotta go" or something equally corny. We said 'bottoms up" finished off our drinks, exchanged a few more tales and headed out for home. There was probably a darn good chance that old PK had sat in one of those old stools downing a cool one spinning a yarn or two. We couldn't wait to tell the rest of the Butler clan of our back country adventures. Think we would have made our Papa proud.

THE LADY MIZPAH & TONOPAH TOWN

It had been a few years since I'd been back to Tonopah that summer I met up with my mother at the old Mizpah Hotel. My bus from Reno pulled up to the high stepping sidewalk and I found Miss Ella sitting in the near empty hotel having a beer.

I teased her about getting married in that place so long ago-1947 in the middle of Winter. She grinned and gave her number two daughter a big hug. We stayed awhile chatting with the bar keep and one of the workers. The Mizpah was not as grand as in her 1908 debut but was hanging in there. Amid rumors she had a few ghosts keeping residence in the old palace. Some folks were so intrigued they brought in paranormal experts. Never having seen the visitors myself(and glad of it)I'm not sure what to believe.

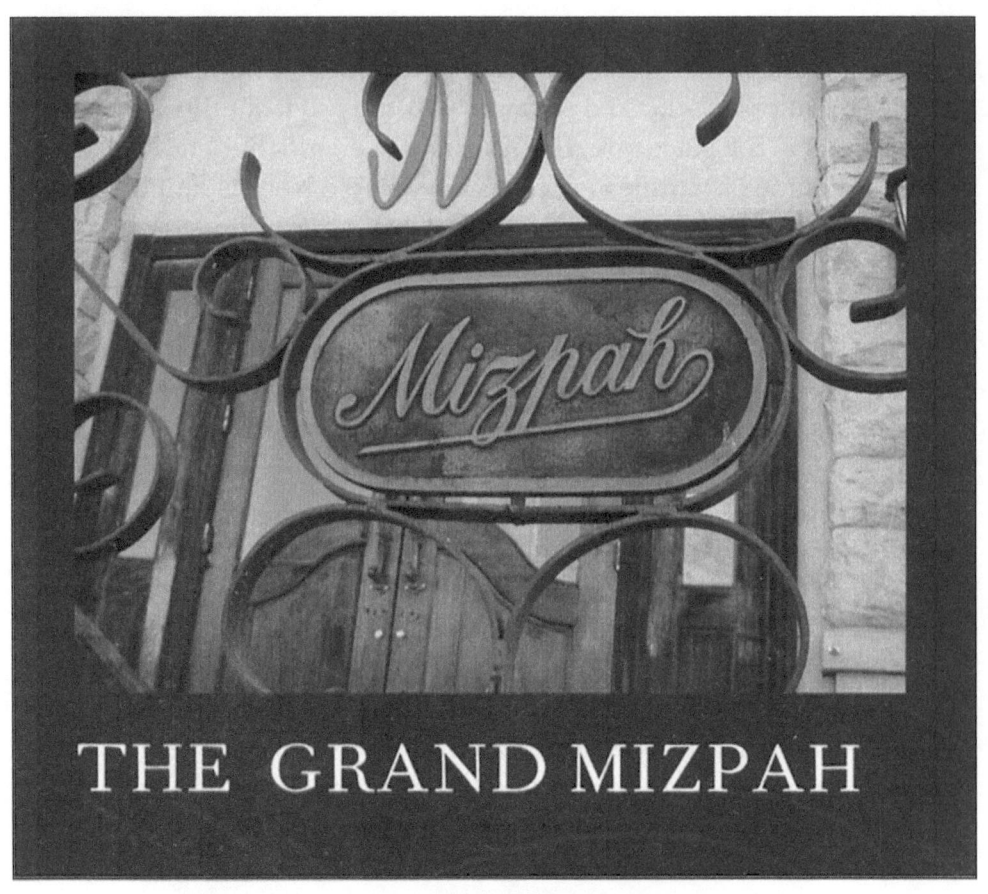

THE GRAND MIZPAH

The Historic Mizpah Hotel in her New Glory
Photo by
Sue Stoutenburg

Later she would get two chances for a new chapter in her amazing history. The first would come in 1980 when Frank Scott(Las Vegas businessman) would swoop in and restore the historic lady to her former glory. Her renaissance would not last many years and eventually she would be boarded up and on the selling block again. Decades later Nancy and Fred Cline purchased the grand Lady to honor Nancy's ancestral roots. The grand re-opening in 2011 had to be pretty close to the lavish party thrown in 1908 when the Mizpah first opened her doors. Champagne was flowing, feasting was on the caliber of an elegant San Francisco café and there was good old country music filling up the rafters.

The beveled glass windows were sparkling and the front halls full of fancy velvet settees -the wood bar in full operation once again after a long dry spell. Part of the Butler clan stayed in the Belle & Jim Butler suite and all were wined and dined like queens and kings. The only thing missing was P.K. standing in the middle of it all bursting with stories of his colorful (step)grandfather and grandmother. Giving his grandson(the first boy in his branch of the Butler family) an earful of tall tales. After a few cool beers it's likely there'd be a sample of some two-stepping and an old song or two PK style.

Even across the miles with the big mountains between us I can still picture Miss Tonopah. The fresh dust circling on a warm summer afternoon when the sun is heating up over the wide desert soil. I can hear the whir of the big semi-trucks passing through on the main highway that runs through town. I can envision the old men standing watch outside the famous Mizpah Hotel taking in the whole kit and kaboodle. Hear the hum of those noisy little slot machines pouring out the open windows of the casino palaces.

The back yards and alleys filled with relics of another time and place. Rusted up and carrying hidden clues to a past life.

I never saw Miss Tonopah in her heyday so I can only imagine her then. It's hard to picture her smothered in champagne and all gussied up. A lot of folks like her rough and ready. A true reminder of the old west days. Even Wyatt and Josie Earp and the famous fighter Jack Dempsey spent time in the little mining town. That must account for something on the authenticity scale.

Everywhere you look you know what she always was and is today. An old mining town. Not quite forgotten but she has known more prosperous days. Still there's a lot of her spirit left. In the old mine shacks and wooden cabins. More than likely home to a few broken dreams. Every tin bucket and shattered bottle has a story to tell.

My hat goes off to all those dedicated townsfolk who have not only kept her alive but didn't 'ruin' her as my papa would say. She wears her age pretty well when you think of all that she's been up against. Miss Tonopah takes on all the stories of all those who pass through and becomes more of what she might have been.

Some say she had a destiny. This little City so rich in earthen treasures. Gold and glitter are rarely of the lasting sort. Likely everyone who had high hopes for her knew that sacred truth. The glory days could not last forever. Could another part-time prospector kick up another "rags to riches" tale before her days are done? Stranger things have happened in this crazy world.

When the last of the old-timers pass on to the Big House in the sky she will lose a little of her color. Perhaps seem a wee bit too tame and quiet. Then one day another lively cowpoke will ride into town in his worn out pickup truck. The tumbleweeds blowing and the sun shining bright on the little mining camp that helped revive the

Nevada economy and rebuild San Francisco after the Big Strike in 1900. There are yet new stories to burst forth in this tiny village that's had more comebacks than Howard Hughes (who has a bit of history here too). There was a bomber base built in 1942 and later turquoise mining exploded and in more recent years a boom in solar energy and the trucking industry gave the town a shot of adrenaline.

New buckets of prosperity could spill over onto the old sidewalks and dusty rock piles. When the next rich ore surfaces or another western adventure puts Miss Tonopah smack dab in the big spotlight yet again. In the meantime Tonopah has a great museum at the edge of town(Central Nevada Museum) that has a fascinating collection of vintage photographs, old mining artifacts, old west history and historic Native American and pioneer memorabilia. Another great stop is the Tonopah Historic Mining Park where you can go underground and step into the very mines that produced millions of dollars in rich ore back in the early 1900's. The park covers more than 100 acres.

Part time prospector Jim Butler and his wife Belle may have founded this small town and stirred up the silver and gold dust but she now belongs to anyone who has called her home. Who carried her voice into the light of day and fought her battles. Working from sun-up to sundown to keep their Town going. They are the ones who kept her alive and kicking. Like the rest of the old west wandering club I'm proud to know her. Proud to walk her streets and recall all the pages of history that have unfolded under God's watchful eye.

All Around Cowboy Richie Minaberry with
The Winning Saddle 1950's ~Bishop

Chapter 8

Rodeo Richie & Benton Rosie

Most people lead two separate lives in their time on this earth. The one they live in the outside world and that other one. In the inner chambers. I knew my Uncle Richie had a big universe beyond our old house and small town and big mountains.

In most ways he belonged to the dusty physical and thrilling world of the cowboy more than his blood kin or jobs(to pay for rodeo-ing & rent). Still I knew he was second only to our parents in how much he loved us and expected big things for us.

Some times it felt like we lived in the shadow of his other lives. Other moments it felt like we as his nieces and nephew moved to dead center.

I understand it all better now through a woman's eyes. Having gone down some of those same roads as an Auntie. To a ten year old it was a big mystery. A foreign puzzle not to be figured out or fit together. Richard Minaberry spoke of horses like most folks talk about their children. The massive creatures were his north and south. His breath, his heart and part of his tangled up roots. That lie beneath the grand Sierras and the White mountain range. Folks might say he was a part-time cowboy-rodeo man but there was nothing part time about it. Every waking moment he was not driving around in his Union Oil truck making deliveries Richie could be found at the corrals roping, riding and grooming his horses.

Almost all of his pals were cowpokes to boot. The assorted lot spoke a different language-had a certain uniform –worn in blue jeans and cowboy shirts with the required topping off- a properly seasoned cowboy hat. Most of the women Richie grew fond of over the years came tied to the end of one of those beautiful four legged beasts as well. For who could understand his deep con-suming passion more than a woman who had horse fever as well. His cowgirls could talk their handsome, dark wavy haired cowboy into an evening of dancing at the Beacon or fairgrounds likely due to the fact that things at the stables were pretty quiet at night.

Not to mention like many of his cowpoke bent he liked a cool one now and again and the next best thing to riding horses was talking horses. Richie was a man's man in a lot of ways but with a gentle soul. He loved kids and since he didn't have any of his own his nieces and nephew got a lot of his sweet affection and good na-tured kidding and jokester ways.

After a stint in the service-not rough duty in Hawaii(a soldier's dream) he stuck pretty close to home. Except for following rodeos around the west and a few trips with his buddy Jim to the grand nationals at the Cow Palace.

The high point of his rodeo life was winning the All Around Cowboy Award at the Bishop Rodeo on homecoming week-end in the 1950's. In his fancy western shirt and new Levi's and looking mighty fine in his big black cowboy hat he had a grin as big as a chevy truck across his face. I was too young to remember that day. My sisters and I have looked at the worn photograph so many times we kind of feel like we were there.

The prize was a magnificent hand tooled saddle and silver buckle. They would become his proudest possession.

One of Richie's best pals Jim Koch remembers the cowboys and their friend Jack flying down the road in Richie's new Chevy. Headed for the grand national rodeo at the famous Cow Palace. The Bishop country boys painted the town-big city style that weekend before it was time for the rodeo fellows to pack up and make the trek over the high passes towards home. A painted memory that would last a lifetime.

Richie never did settle down with just one woman though he came very close. He had a few broken hearts along the rodeo highway. We had our favorites and kept in touch with Miss D. long after the smoke cleared from their romance. It didn't seem in the cards for Richie to put his eggs in that marriage basket. Not so terrible for us for we got a bigger piece of him that we didn't have to share with anyone. Still I felt a little sad he didn't start a family of his own watching many of his rodeo buddies getting hitched and having babies.

In the fall of 1966 Richie had been struggling with a whole bucket of health issues and had gone to a hospital in Reno for surgery. He would never ride another spirited pony across an open field. We got the call one Sunday afternoon he was gone.

He was thirty six years old and that was one of the darkest days of my life. It took me a long time to say goodbye. Even longer to let the sweet memories wrap around me like a Grandma quilt. Now nearly fifty years later I only recall the best days. Of watching our handsome uncle carry the flag down Main Street in the big Labor Day Homecoming parade.

Seeing him hang on for dear life to a crazy bull doing his darnedest to buck off that cowboy. The big grins and deep belly laughter when his girls were tickling him and the bear hugs that made everything seem like it was going to be alright(when you kind of knew it wasn't).

My one regret is that I didn't become the cowgirl I know he would have loved for me to be(thankfully my sister Sundown & cousin Andy followed in the cowboy footsteps). Due to raw fear of those massive animals and some fat allergies that left me swollen eyed and sneezing fits.

I hope he understood. I would've given anything to make him proud. Maybe writing a few tales of the wild west and the cowgirls and cowpokes who worked to tame it might just be enough to say thanks for the "memories" to my favorite cowboy.

Benton Rosie

That sweet smell of orange pie hit your nose the minute you walked into Rosie's little Café on the old Highway 6 road headed for Reno & Tonopah. The place was hardly bigger than a roomy closet but big enough for weary travelers and home town folks to sit a spell and get some good finger licking grub. Most comers couldn't resist the melt in your mouth pies topped off with an ice cold Coca-cola or a tangy bottle of orange soda.

Miss Rosie had a big smile for everybody who walked through those doors. Be they complete strangers or longtime pals. Her rosy cheeks and big grin lit up that Café like a thousand watt bulb. It was contagious too.

Most folks left that place smiling like a new mama bird. You couldn't nurse a case of the "feeling sorry for yourself" malady when you were hanging out at Rosies'. It wasn't just the home cooking like your Mama used to make. It was a happy place filled with good smells, deep laughter and a feeling of home. As corny as it sounds that Café seemed to be bursting out with the sweet fragrance of love. Rosie had about enough of that stuff to go around for every-one in the whole darn country I believe.

An Old Cowpoke~ Full of Stories
Benton, California

Most every Saturday afternoon Old Pete would stop in at Rosie and Porky's Café and Gas Station in new Benton on his way back from Bishop town. His old blue and white station wagon(that doubled as the school bus Monday through Friday) would be full to the brim with supplies from Joseph's market. Porky would gas up old Betsy(as Pete called his jitney) to have her ready for Monday morning pick-up duty.

I learned a lot about life in that little café watching Old Pete and Rosie and her Porky talk about old times and good cooking. There wasn't anything they wouldn't do for their Basquo buddy.

When we grand-kids tagged along we got the royal treatment too. We'd feel extra proud sitting on the stool next to our big Grandpa drinking a tall orange soda.

Grandpa Pete wasn't a big talker so Rosie kinda did the talking for the both of them. She'd tease her Basquo pal a bit and give us all the news from around town. You didn't need local tv news back then. You had your own ace reporters like Rosie and Cowboy Conway to do the job.

When Old Pete said it was time to go we sure hated to leave. Old Pete would pull out his wallet out of his bib overalls and pay up with some crisp dollar bills. Rosie would hand off one of those famous orange pies and off we'd go headed for Benton Station a few miles up the road.

I couldn't wait to taste that first bite. It was beyond description.

As old Pete pulled onto the highway and we waved good-bye to Rosie and Porky I felt as sad as if I'd lost my best friend. One couldn't find that kind of welcome just any place down the road. We knew it'd be pretty quiet in Old Benton at the Minaberry House. Without Rosie's sugar sweet smile even if we did have her special pie to remember her by.

Old Abe ~ Selling his Wares at the Adobes
Santa Fe, New Mexico

Chapter 9

Beyond the Sierra Trail

The Sacred Songs of Santa Fe

There is no place that will ever hold my heart as my Sierra Valley. It was my first and forever Homeland. Though one summer I landed in a Holy Place that stirred something river deep and wide in this country woman.

I am not the first or last soul to fall for the azure blue skies and pinon tree lands of Santa Fe, New Mexico. It has much in common with my Sierra soil. Air as pure and fragrant as sweet Heaven. The dry bones and empty boots of the old west alive and well in the shadow of the Native American sovereign territory. Much like the earthen paradise of my ancestors the Sangre de Cristo Mountains are holy temples. Painted in ivory dust in the winter solstice and those purple grey mountains of majesty looking lovely under the seasons of the Mother Sun. The "Summer of My Santa Fe" came from some notes I wrote on my second trip to New Mexico. I had fully lost myself in her sacred spell. I rented a little Casita near town and the creative juices poured out of me like a rushing river.

"She gazed out at the little garden from the big casita window. Drinking in the earthy smooth adobe like a hungry fawn. A tall fragrant pinon stands near the main house like a green wooden tower reaching towards the blue water color sky. The sound of morning birds rise through the side window. Hamill had never set eyes on this place before. Never walked the stone path leading out into the summer air past the August roses(that reminded her of her mother's garden). How can it be that her mind breathes the air of true home. As though she'd woken up under those sturdy pine beams every day of her young life. Truth was she'd only passed through this Santa Fe town once. She fell hard and fast. If not for her Montgomery waiting behind in San Francisco Hamill would have told them to pack all her worldly goods and send them on the next truck headed for New Mexico. In the steel cold blue reality she knew she'd seen the town through new eyes that first time. On her Sunday best. Still when it came time to go the leaving burnt a little hole inside of her. The road not taken etched on her summer mind. Time passed and as with all things the red hot passion faded some. The fire never going out.

Something in that land called her back. To that little mound of clay covered earth. That blue corn sky. Those sweet brown adobes melting into distant hills and strong pinons. As though they were one with the clouds and the stars on the far horizon. Hamill had traveled long and away to the land of her Basque ancestors and walked the streets of Paris and New York. No place had claimed her the way this Land had done. It was as though she was under a spell and had no power over it. Hamill found an ad for a little casita in the local newspaper. It was a little over her budget but something in her said 'you must stay'. Her prayers answered. To get back to her center of gravity and nurture the artist inside before it was too late.

And so she stayed a long month of Sundays to get to know this beautiful Lady not as a stranger but as a lost woman come home.

In the evenings she would walk along the Plaza in town. The soft light of nightfall dancing on the smooth stone --the cobblestones glistening. The tall towers of St. Francis lighting the dark sky. Her first evening a soft desert rain fell on the red earth.

Little drops of fresh mother earth wine tickled her face as she remembered that sweet sage smell of a mountain storm from her childhood.

Later the August moon shone brightly over the adobe shops and cafés. A soft glow over the square told her this was a holy place. It caught her breath. The whole taste of it. The warm croon of a folk singer filled the night air.

The place had changed some since her first visit a handful of summers ago. Yet the tranquil spirit had remained ever present.

That summer of her Santa Fe she unleashed her creative gates wide and deep open. She didn't understand it all and perhaps never would but she belonged to this Land in a way she had only been tied to one other place. Her Sierra mountains and treasured Owens Valley.

Hamill smiled thinking it quite permissible to love two places in your life. Those who lose themselves in an earthen paradise are the blessed ones. This had become her Santa Fe. That did not mean she need own it. Or that she must take a piece of it to call her own. To carry the holy ground and moon lit sky somewhere inside would be enough.

There is something to be said for a sacred place that remains in your city mind. To color a dark winter's day or hold the scent of sage in the still air. The Lady of Santa Fe seems to have it all. The feast of the seasons. The raw rhythms of Mother Earth. That big watercolor blue canvas sky. The ancient voices of the brown and white ancestors who lived and died on this holy soil.

As morning broke on her eleventh day Hamill pondered whether she could drink it in day by day until her mind was full of the sound and sense of it all. So that when the summer of her Santa Fe ended she could carry it with her. God had brought her to this sacred place to find peace. To make her remember what it was to re-claim your soul. After too long away."

The Golden Lady By The Bay

Some roads west lead to bigger towns off the long and traveled highways. Where you might have to dig a little deeper to find gold. San Francisco is one of those places where you can pass through and see only the shiny and new. The glitz and the dazzle. Missing all the old world charm and the deep caverns of history that re-main alive and well in this amazing phoenix who rose from the ashes in the 1906 Earthquake and Fire. A vibrant mix of cultures, new transplants and old families who have called her home for long generations.

The old girl's past is painted on every street corner. They can fancy her up but still the Foundation on which this City was built will rise up from the stunning ivory dome of City Hall to the majestic Palace of Fine Arts to the sky high arms of that masterful Golden Gate.

Until the last light goes out on this western jewel she will shine bright as the north star at midnight. She's still got a lot of living to do and a whole lot of history to boast about before the curtain falls.

For starters there's John's Grill a fine little restaurant near Market Street and the hustle and bustle of downtown. Where the famous mystery writer Dashiell Hammett hung out. While penning some of the great lively twisted tales of the 1930's and 40's.(Maltese Falcon was one-later made into a movie starring Humphrey Bogart) There was a little real life intrigue a few years back when a replica of the Maltese Falcon was stolen from owner John Konstin's famous San Francisco eatery on Ellis Street. After long months with 'no clues' Konstin proceeded to have another replica built to replace the missing bird. The historic restaurant has been deemed a national literary Landmark for Hammett's loyal patronage and presence during his prolific writing days.

THE REMEMBRANCE

For years John's Grill hosted the Earthquake Survivor's dinner on April 18th. It was a touching affair watching Mr. Herbert and Josephine and all the Ladies nearing the 100 year mark be wined and dined and given the royal treatment by the City who honors her past. It was thrilling to be standing at the early morning ceremony with old police cars and fire engines sirens blazing as they ushered off the Earthquake gang to the St. Francis for their 1906 commemorative breakfast. One lady was heard to say "It's the very best day of the year". In the wee hours of the morning the City still in the dark cloak of night a wreath was laid at Lotta's Fountain to honor the dead. Standing there my mind went to my own ancestors.

Belle and Jim Butler were staying at the Russ Hotel in town for mining business when the earth opened up. They were two blessed to survive the devastating shaker. I thought of the horrors they must have seen as they walked dazed around the streets of rubble and bodies looking for a horse to hire to get home to San Jose. Auntie Elma who lived with the Butlers in the San Jose house said she remembered Belle and Jim coming down the street in a wagon driven by one horse. Jim's legs dangling over the back. Jim was able to hire the driver for $75. To bring the couple the near fifty miles south to the House on 14th street. A long buggy ride normally and with the roads torn up even a rougher journey. Their anxious children were greatly relieved to see them. It surely was a day that changed San Francisco and everyone who lived through it.

If those historic spots don't knock your socks off stop in at Saint Peter and Paul's Church(built 1924) across from Washington Square Park where the young DiMaggio brothers played a little baseball with kids from the old neighborhood. Or stand on Market Street by the Palace Hotel where the great opera singer-Enrico Caruso was staying when the big 1906 Quake hit and nearly destroyed this great City. A Town that gave us Poet Robert Frost, Author Jack London, Dancer Isadora Duncan, Levi's and delicious sourdough bread(among other equally important inventions) did not buckle under adversity but rather rose above it.

Where else could you find a five star restaurant down the street from an old boarding house Basque Hotel and café where you could eat a ten course meal for under twenty dollars. Or the local's favorite Red's Java House a little eatery in a tiny shed that still sells hamburgers for under $5.00. With one of the best views in Town of the Bay bridge and the working waterfront (not the fancy panoramic vistas).

Echoes of the Old Voices of San Francisco
Circle the Air
Palace of Fine Arts
Photo by
Melissa Rosno

The big ships seem close enough to touch and the brave Bay crews that keep everything ship shape down under the Bay and above board as well - will be right there beside you devouring a burger and fries and an old fashioned cup of joe.

The Obrero

If you wanted a little European flavor and there's lot of it in this City a stop in at The Obero Hotel in the middle of Chinatown in the 1980's would've been just the ticket.

A single room cost a whopping $35 —was homey and spit polished. It was kind of farmhouse style with the bathroom down the hall. Bambi MacDonald was the proprietor a formidable woman who cooked up a storm in her little kitchen. Though she was not Basque you'd never know it from her sumptuous meals. There were about ten courses and wine for about $10.00 give or take a dollar or two. She served things up family style so you never knew who your dining companions might be that night.

That added to the charm. Bambi is no longer with us and took most of her recipes with her but even the memory of those fragrant dishes makes my mouth water some twenty years later.

San Francisco is the City that knows how-most of the time. The Town that gave us the prolific Herb Caen who knew more about that City's history than Gene Autry knew about cowboys. Herb and I exchanged a few notes back and forth. His witty weapon of choice- An old manual typewriter that did not have one bit or byte or download button.

The City of St Francis was a particular favorite in our family. The only City in the world that could hold a candle to his beloved mountains my Father, Uncle Bob and Cousin Helen and various other assorted relatives loved her like nobody's business. Easy to see why she's the hardest City in the world to leave behind. I know. I've been trying for nearly 20 years.

The Old Butler Hotel in Big Pine, California ~A Great Place
to Bed Down & Dine in the Beautiful Sierras
(Photo by Harry W. Mendenhall) circa 1914.

Chapter 10

Open Lands & True Rivers

One cold December afternoon we took a ride out highway 6 with sister number three. For another look at our Irish great-grandparents' Ranch in Hamill Valley. The rolling hills off to the east were painted with fresh glistening snow. The white ice can be so forgiving. A soft blanket covering rock and sage and tree stubs. Forgiving of barren dirt roads and bare winter poplars. In your mind it was as though you'd been set down in a Currier and Ives Christmas card. You almost gave in to humming Rosemary Clooney's version of White Christmas (Irving Berlin 1942).

There are fields of open land between the scattered ranches. We spotted the narrow road to the old Hamill Ranch and turned under the poplar trees showing a bit of age. A few worn down sheds sat amidst the old cottonwoods and winter sagebrush. A vivid reminder of another time. When William Hamill and his wife and brothers fresh from Ireland worked hard to tame the soil and raise livestock and children. With the sweat of their hands.

A small pond ran quiet and smooth near the old wood shed. Likely an offspring of the snow run-offs. Welcome just the same in the land of little rain. We walked out to the old road that led to the highway. A long buggy wide path lined with the tall poplars that helped tame the winds. I imagined William and Mary riding back

Peavine Ranch in Nevada~~1950
Charlie & Marian Keough's Welcoming Hacienda for
Wandering Relatives & Friends

from town or church. Their small children restless in their Sunday clothes. Ready to spill out as soon as the horses pulled into the barn. I had never known this land as my own. I was just a visitor passing through like so many before me. William Hamill met with a grisley end in this Territory but I wasn't going to hold that against the place. Darkness can call on any town.

In any time. I wanted to remember the better days. Of an Irish father and his brother. Building a strong house fit for any Sierra winter that might burst in. His young bride putting away food for the long days of winter in between sewing and cooking and tending to the small children.

It was not just their story. It was the story of every immigrant or stranger who came to tame the land on their own terms. Some found out mighty quick-that land would not be so easily tamed.

There was a metal sign down the Lane that spelled out Hamill Road. The only true mark left behind of the Irish family who were torn apart. By death and trouble. The descendants of William and Mary are spread out across the Owens Valley, Nevada and Beyond. They carry the immigrant pioneer blood into the new century. Voices and Children rising from the ashes and dust

The Big H Farm

After living in San Francisco for some years I was itchy to get back to the country life. To open fields and back roads that lead nowhere. We found if we went a little farther out we got a little more house for the money. A good thing for our first house.

In Napa town there was a little farm stand at the end of our street. That spring I bought my first tomato plant determined to be a farmer in progress. Fighting with the clay soil in our backyard we got off to a bumpy start. From my office window upstairs we had a panoramic view of the Napa hills and a working farm run by the local high school. It was a regular Old McDonalds operation with an assortment of pigs, horses, sheep and a few grazing cows. We'd hit the jackpot. It seemed life couldn't get any better.

It did get better. We were blessed to meet up with a farming duo who took the city dwellers under their wings and tried to teach us everything they had stored in their heads. About earth tending. What we mostly learned was that we'd grown too soft for that hardworking, back bending work but it was pretty fun to fantasize growing a big vegetable garden in our new(albeit small patch of earth). At the end of the summer we took inventory. We produced exactly six tiny carrots, 2 watermelons the size of quarters and two stalks of corn that looked finger size and a cabbage plant that kept thriving that we planted by accident.

We decided rather wisely to leave the farming to the true professionals after that summer.

John and Margaret Hoffman ran their family farm just a couple of miles down the road. From the very first moment we stepped on that fertile land we sensed it was an enchanted place. Next to the old barn and farm sheds we had a strong sensation of coming home.

It felt hauntingly familiar to the detective and the writer who grew up around family farms in the Sierras & the back county of Virginia. A country lane that led visitors into the Big H farm took me back to the dirt path from busy Main Street into my grandfather's ranch in Bishop Town(California). The old farmhouse from the 1800's sat across from the big weathered barn. Farmer John gave us a grand tour of the place and we saw that we were in farm heaven as rows and rows of fruit trees called out to us. A country girl's dream. A vision of my sisters and I out in the side orchard picking the rosy red apples of fall on our grandfathers' ranch came back to me. Taking that first crisp taste of the sweet juice was a thrill then and thirty some years later equally as exciting. It soothes something primal in those of us who live off the grocery store shelves.

You can go home again it seems. Only sometimes we find home in a different place than where we left it. Miles away and with tall mountains in between-the faces changed but it was a new sense of home nonetheless.

After the big farm tour we would be invited into the inner sanctum at the newer farm house the Hoffmans had built in more recent years. This would become a favorite ritual over the next decade. First you take a look at what's growing around the farm and fill your bags full of whatever was ready for picking. Farmer John would encourage a quick taste of the luscious French prunes and sweet apricots straight off the branch and usually join his guests in the testing. Then into the house we'd go for some of Margaret's fresh lemon, pear or apple pie prepared from fresh picked goods that afternoon.

A feast for the culinary senses indeed. It was rather like going into a time machine. The big table covered in a lovely patchwork quilt and Miss Margaret's canning cupboard off towards the hall. Filled to the brim with the summer's crop that would keep her brood in tasty fruits and veggies most of the long Winter months. We would while away the Saturday afternoon talking farming or other green subjects or share our travel stories(the 90 plus years they'd been on earth they'd jaunted all over the world) or a little dabble in politics(throw the bums out was heard a time or two). Not only was Farmer John always at the ready with a hearty lesson on earth tending and simple living (this place was more green than the San Francisco mint) but he and Miss Margaret could teach us all a bit about partnerships.

The couple worked side by side planning and plotting their dreams for more years than many have been alive. In 1949 they bought a piece of prime land-23 acres in all In the lush Napa Valley when prunes were Queen(later the area would explode with grape vineyards). It was on that soil they would begin their family. The road would take a few detours along the way but they held onto the Farm through lean days and challenging times. In the new millennium their great grandchildren come from all over the country to follow Grandpa John around the farm. Listening to his stories of planting and his turn to organic, dry farming to take better care of his patch of earth. The young folks stop in the little fruit stand store in an old shed that has fed more families fresh produce than the big chain store down the street. Then after a peek at John's amazing bonsai tree collection the Hoffman crew will pop into the kitchen café where Margaret had fresh walnut bars and cold drinks waiting. They might talk their great grandma into reciting one of her delightful poems and take a peek at her yearly diaries that chronicle the daily goings on at the Hoffman plot. It does a heart good to watch this duo. Both in their 90's age has worn them down a bit physically as it is known to do but their spirits are strong and full of youthful nectar. Their friend Jean used to proclaim "they still hold hands after all these years. Still crazy about each other. For as they planted seeds and orchards this blessed duo planted buckets of affection and laughter - two ingredients sure to grow the finest of crops.

Our "brother of the trees" as John was referred to on occasion seemed to have taken up where John Muir left off. Get him talking about old oak trees or tall sequoias and his eyes began to twinkle. His face would take on a golden glow –without a doubt this was his life passion. (The two Johns would meet up in a sense. John Hanna-Muir's grandson tended his family vineyard across town from the Hoffman Farm and they came to know one another through their local Napa Church)

One summer afternoon we were loaded down with bags of the sweet produce from the Big H orchard. Saying good-bye in front of the weathered barn we mentioned we were headed to Santa Barbara that week-end to meet the family. Well John got that silvery glint in his eyes, his voice raised up an octave and we knew something was up. With some sort of hybrid energy running through his body he called out "Hey you've got to take a look at that old oak by the train station. It's a real beauty. Been there for years"(if not for my sporadic memory I'd recite her exact vintage which John surely told us).

So a few days later with our whole brood in tow we trekked over to the train station and carried out our duty. That ancient oak was amazing up close. I passed her a hundred times on my way to somewhere and sadly had barely noticed her. The massive trunk and the graceful thick wooded branches stretched out for what seemed like miles.

Painted with emerald green leaves the giant oak resembled a beautiful sculpture you might happen upon in one of those fancy Chicago or New York museum gardens.

This was the unique thing about Mr. Hoffman and his sweetheart of near seventy years. They had that uncanny knack of making you see things anew. To guide those foolish folks rushing through life to put on the brakes. To not only smell the flowers but to plant a few. Finding the Farm plus an amazing adopted family at the end of that northern road wove pieces of our past into the rich soil of the new valley we called home. The living breathing parcel of sacred history the Hoffmans kept watch over (the land had once been owned by the famous Vallejo family) made us feel as though we had deep dug in roots as well. It was not an accident we had come to this Valley and this town. We were led there surely as sheep are guided to their grazing lands. A blessing of the long west road from the high Sierras and old Virginia to yet another chance at finding home.

The Old Hoffman Farm-"Best Darn Peaches & Plums"
in the Whole Valley
Napa Valley, California
Photo by RM Lacy

Wooden Houses

THE HOUSE ON BROCKMAN LANE

We grew up in the big rambling house that sat beneath the shadow of Mt. Tom down the street from Brockman's Corner Market & Gas Station on Highway 395.

There were five of us; three daughters under age twelve and Mama and Papa. Almost all of our important life lessons took place on that half-acre of land in the Owens Valley nestled under the grand Sierra Mountain range.

For years folks called it the Butler House. Some still do though our family hasn't lived there for years. It still feels like our house. People still ask my sisters about the place when we're in town. The place hasn't changed much from the outside anyway. There's a few more trees and the shrubs have grown up pretty high but it's close to how I remember her.

Now there is no smell of garlic coming from the direction of the old kitchen at the back of the house. Something good was always cooking on the big stove when Mama was around. Father won't be seen in the back shed while he tends to his onery buck "Big Boy" and other assorted critters.

As kids we used to feel a bit disappointed by that old house. As though she should have stayed ours forever. Her old cupboards always full of our family keepsakes and dishes.

It seems much like your first love. You never fall as deeply for another house as you did for the one you most remember and loved.

Growing older we realized it was just ordinary walls of wood and plaster but it was that those rooms held the pieces of our past. The voices of our grandfather and Uncles and Cousins lost to us now. No other place will carry those cherished sounds again.

Philip P. Keough House off Main Street in
Bishop, California (early 1900's)
(lft to rt) Family Friend, Edna Keough
& her father Philip P. Keough

It wasn't really a fancy house though it was an old Victorian with a high winding staircase and dark mahogany trim. We didn't have the budget to spruce it up a lot but It suited us just fine a little worn around the edges.

Unexpected guests who happened along were welcomed with father's own brand of hospitality. Some form of libation was always on hand and visitors were usually invited to stay for supper if it was ok with Mama. There always seemed to be room for one more at the table. Though we were far from rich I don't think anyone ever left the table hungry.

As is true of most places we live in not all the memories of that old house were happy ones. Death and illness came to call far too often. I sought refuge behind the big player piano when our dear Uncle Richie died.

News came of other friends and family lost to us. It was in that front room where our family gathered and cried together when President Kennedy was shot. For days we sat blurry eyed and huddled close. Feeling a bit safer in our little cocoon. They were the best of times and the worst of times. But we made it through together. The five of us our assorted pooches and that wonderful old house that had come to seem like a cherished old friend.

The Town Ranch

Our father, his two brothers and one sister grew up on the Keough Butler Ranch off Main Street in Bishop Town. It was a grand rambling old house built by P.P. Keough Superintendent of the Wells Fargo Company. In the early 1900's P.P. Keough started development of Keough's Hot Springs recreation resort with a large pool & hot baths and cabins. The Owens Valley pioneer also owned the Keough's market on Main St. in the Ben Franklin Store building(still standing).

The Town Ranch was the site of numerous family gatherings to celebrate weddings and birthdays and the less happy occasions as funerals and sending soldiers off to war(all Three sons served during WWII).

The House had a wonderful big old fashioned farm house kitchen perfect for cooking up elaborate feasts and family suppers. Off to the right of the kitchen there was a long rock cellar that sat behind the screened in front porch. It was a great place for exploring. It was set up like a little general store with rows of food supplies and cooking utensils. Sturdy mixing bowls and baking pans lined up in a row ready to go. There was a full dining room towards the front of the house next to the side porch. The shelves were lined with fancy glass goblets and painted china. It was a room you treaded lightly so as not to break anything.

There was a little parlor near the side porch where PK's mother kept her writing desk and ceramic bird collection. The big bay windows let a lot of sunshine in and you could see the little sparrows playing in the garden. It seemed grand to have a whole little room just for writing and reading.

The upstairs was like a whole house to itself. You climbed up the steep scary steps and there were a couple of small bedrooms leading to the huge room kept by PK's parents. It had a wood stove and sitting area along with a big high poster bed.

PK said the kids used to sneak up the back stairs(that ran outside the house) when they were grounded or in a bit of trouble.

There was a stone pond near the long trellis walkway at the front of the house. On warm summer evenings and spring afternoons this would be the gathering place for greeting long lost relatives and friends who'd stopped in for a visit.

There were a number of outbuildings as well as two large barns on the property. A little garden full of cherry tomatoes and beans and other summer fare flourished by the hay barn. There was a huge apple orchard in the field near the old Catholic Church. Where PK and his girls picked the sweet fruit in the fall for applesauce and pie making.

There were lilies of the valley all down the driveway leading into the Ranch and dark green holly bushes that PK took cuttings from every Christmas. It was an enchanting place hidden behind poplar trees and high bushes from the rest of the world.

Like a mysterious Chateau-the empty rooms seemed like there might be a few friendly ghosts roaming around. How we wished we had known her in her heyday-the rooms filled with happy noise and all the assorted colorful ancestors. If only those walls could talk. What stories they could tell.

Last Leaves of Fall in Sierras

Chapter 11

Sacred Seasons

I often wonder if the season of our birth can influence those months we most identify with in our earthly journey. Being born in the deep of November fall is the season when every fiber of my being comes alive.

A Sierra spring is an awesome sight with the sweet lilacs bursting out for their brief fragrant dance. The blanket of wild irises spreading across the fields and the first daffodils peeking out from the brown soil. This was our mother's treasured time. The days of winter had stood long and hard and the taste of spring brought many back to life.

Mama's first look at the world was in the deep of winter. Perhaps that accounted for the season of blooms and sunshine holding such a magic power over her. Having been blessed to travel about and experience the glory of autumn in many places across the country it only confirmed my belief that the Owens Valley stood her ground.

Waved the yellow flag as the rows of cottonwoods and aspen trees burst into golden flame on both the Valley floor and near the edge of the awesome range of Sierra Nevada's.

A luminous glow come late September or mid-October hand in hand with the clear blue open sky and crisp clean high country air painting a photographer's dream.

Some decry the burst of fall for all too soon the iridescent leaves come soaring to Earth. Signaling the hard face of winter is close behind. Perhaps that deep sense of hunger knowing we must wait another handful of seasons to taste our own infusion is what stirs the magic pot. Could it be that the red hot anticipation gets us through the ordinariness of colorless days.

Stone Creeks & Favorite Mountain Watering Holes

One of the treasured places to hear the rushing creeks and the seasonal dance of color was up the hill from Bishop Town at Tom's Place. That old cabin café and general store holds a bucket of memories for the Butler girls. Anytime Papa was on 395 going north. We knew PK's pickup was due to stop in either going or coming. Tom's Place was one of Papa's favorite watering holes. In Bishop Town the gathering place was McMurrys Saloon run by the McMurry brothers (Ray and Lloyd) an old Owens Valley family.

Like McMurrys Tom's Place was a fun spot packed with old pals and ripe stories. I can still see PK sitting on the high barstools-belly up to the bar-grinning from ear to ear. We girls would poke around the general store hoping for a good find for that four bits. Burrowed deep in our blue jean pockets. Then we'd go out by the big creek. That was so loud and powerful you could hardly hear cars going by on the highway. Like a spirited thunderstorm the sound of that water gushing up made us feel so alive - on high octave. There are a few of the old time places still kicking and Tom's Place is one. A true Sierra treasure that's outlasted near a hundred hard winters, a wobbly economy and the dying off of old patrons. Not sure if it's the good chow and ample beer supply. Or that sacred hill where the water runs deep and strong beneath the Sierra peaks.

Whatever keeps them coming back I pray it will be around another hundred summers.

Paradise Lodge

A few years back my sister called and announced they were tearing down Paradise Lodge. It was just as devastating to hear that news as to get word that another old timer had passed on. It was my dream cabin-my fantasy pine lodge. A place of celebration and memory. It was a trip to the mountains without the scary winding roads.

A little bit of paradise just up the road from home. Hidden away in a grove of trees it could not be seen from the highway. The Lodge saw it's fair share of the change of seasons. A palette of color in the middle of October and in the sweet days of summer. The air filled with that delicious woody smell of the mountains. Winter they usually shut down so we missed seeing her in Christmas trim. The stately bar and dining room built of magnificent Sierra pine led this young girl to dream of one day living in a cabin house- An exact replica of the Lodge would do just fine (I'm still waiting).

I heard later there was a reprieve on the tear down −good news. This hall of history closed her doors in 2007. The voices of generations left quiet and still inside those amazing wooden walls.

Like Tom's Place the Lodge had little cabins for rent. Some days we imagined living there by the little creek away from the noise and traffic of town. In reality we wouldn't have lasted long but it was a nice dream just the same.

The wood and stone dwellings of memory became as much a part of our sweet lives as the quaking aspens and rough wooded old cottonwoods. Every leaf and turn in the road seemed like an old friend on the season of return.

In the most barren time the winter solstice it is good to remember that the little seeds are bursting forth beneath the hard frozen ground. God is blessing the sacred lands to bloom again. If all the mornings were true golden or dancing in the nectar of spring. Would we truly treasure them for the magic songs they bring to the thirsty Lands.

A Sierra Christmas

When my mind journeys back to the sacred season of Christmas it is to the Sierras I go. To the ivory frosting painted on the Sierra Range. I picture the blanket of winter laid across the rounded White mountains that stretch along the whole breadth of the Owen's valley. God's Country. A name it so rightly deserves. Whoever first called her by this title knew her well. No land ever fitted the honor more. Over the years I have spent too many holidays away from her. In the sunshine and blue skies of the Bay lands where it doesn't seem so much like Christmas. I drift back to those rugged mountains and starry nights in my December mind. As much as I care for those northern lands her bright lights and festive decorations cannot take the place of a Sierra Christmas.

Where a little girl never gave up that last hope until Christmas morning broke. That the magic snow would arrive on time. Christmas was red hot wood stoves and the smell of pinon burning, warm woolen coats, soft mittens and fuzzy hats. If snow dared not come we would find her. Up the frozen creeks or near the lower peaks. Father would park the green ford on a hard piece of mother earth and off we'd go. Slipping and sliding like happy seals until

Mother gave the sign it was time to go. She knew we would stay until our cheeks were covered with ice if she left us on our own. Papa's three happy girls reluctantly left behind the proud snowman imagining folks would come along to admire our handiwork. We'd beg to take along some of the frosty ice along in a bucket. In our deepest child's heart we knew all the lovely white clouds would melt to mush but it was too hard to say out loud. Looking back I realize how much I hated the snow seeping into my winter jeans turning my blood to ice but we dared not let on for that might be the end of the grand winter adventures.

As December 25th drew near the children would gather at the little Episcopal Church in Bishop (that our great grandfather helped build) for a sweet evening of caroling.

We second and third generation Sierra cherubs belted out the songs of the season with great heart if not strong voices. From house to house we went bundled up tight and bursting with pure glee.

There was a little Christmas train that carried Santa and his elves and the wee folks on a magical ride over fields and snow.

Perhaps the best present of all to the children of the Valley was the lighting of the giant Christmas tree in the town park at the start of the season. It was everything a child could imagine Christmas to be.

Beyond the festive gatherings and winter play lay the amazing backdrop of those tall stone mountains. By day towers of strength and visions of light. By night sacred pillars of sweet heaven touching down to earth.

When you live in a Land so beyond your realm of understanding – far past the reach of the human eye every season is magical. A

Sierra Christmas comes as close in my mind to that holy night of long ago as we may ever know on this earthly land. Her blessed children who must be far away in other lands carry that vision of winters past. From threads of memory. As angels dance for joy upon the silvery peaks.

Chapter 12

The End of This Road

AWAY BUT NEVER GONE

Like most of the human tribe I could not truly appreciate the land where I grew up until I left it behind. At seventeen I was anxious to try my wings and go beyond the borders of my little world. Truth was I was scared to death but I had to know what was out there. Past the long reach of the Sierra Mountains. Having grown up with one movie theater, A Sears catalogue store and a solo radio station(KIBS) that went off the air about ten o'clock. I felt as though I needed to stretch my horizons in the outer universe. To unravel the layers of the big cities and experience tall museums, historic houses and the array of natural wonders. The world was waiting beyond that big door and I wanted to taste it all.

That young girl of seventeen did finish her growing up and did fly away. For a time. Across the highways and back roads of America. Far from her beloved Sierra Mountains. To distant shores of Ireland and the blue –blue waters of the Mediterranean. To the Basque Homeland of her ancestors. But always she found her way home.

Now some nearly forty years later with traveling dust thick on her back she has come to know a raw truth. That she was able to leave her sacred lands behind for she knew it would be there forever. Standing in the wings. Guiding her with a tower of strength. That center of gravity. Her sweet Mama holding down the home fort. Keeping the family safe and strong. Those traveling years were hard on her mother. Times when she couldn't hear her daughter's voice or see her face. Yet her quiet mother endured it all. For she knew she could not stand in the way of a daughter's dreams. The mother was wise to let go-to loosen the reins. For in the end the daughter would return to the Land and the people she belonged to with her complete heart.

Standing on soil far from anything familiar she found no other place could claim her. No other land could fill the empty spaces. She was better for the knowing of it.

Had she never left that home soil she would carry that edge of wonder. That one day would have borne a restlessness inside. That in time could cloud her seeing. Of that holy ground.

The rush of the undiscovered began to fade. The thrill of the chase not gone but lessened. The truth was painted on the open terrain. She belonged to those mountains as much as she would ever belong to any earthly soil. Though all things here are temporary until we leave the world for that final rest. This was her true north.

As it was for her father and his father before him. By morning light and diamonds of darkness. Through thunderous days and icy chill of night. They belonged to this Land. It was here that she would be buried near to her ancestors. Ashes to ashes.

Dust to dust. Beyond all other callings. This is a place called home.

Some Poems

She Lives On

He stood small hands tucked in pockets deep
A quiet boy upon the frozen earth
That claims her now
The matriarch of them all
Dust to dust
Blood to blood
Her spirit tall inside
This half grown boy
His smile carries her own face
Out to the world
And so life does not on this day end
But rather breathes on
Beneath the winter shadows
Of the tall peaks that watched over her
For near a hundred years
She rests now on a passing cloud
Earth to earth
Ashes to ashes
The circle of life
Ties one boy to
The threads of the past
A small wind blows
A chill across his cheek
Time to cross the winter mountains
to find his way to true home

True Rivers

The ancient waters flow in cascading rhythms
Beneath the majestic peaks of power
Sacred oil from holy ground
The lands owe their all to the sparkling liquid
    nectar-agua
Breathing life into species here & gone
Great wars have been declared and
Families split asunder over the river's roaring
    passage
Cities and towns drawing their swords
To claim her now-where shall the true rivers
End in this fierce battle of the crystal drops

As The First Time

Sweet Indian meadow
Glistening blades of laughing grass
Each seeing is the first time
Though memory recalls
Another day
Another song
For a thousand years the
Wild deer and winter bears
Have walked this open land
Yet the soil seems freshly unwrapped
Nearly new
How can it be
In this dark untamed place
The footprints of invisibility
Are as feint as sand
Upon the mother shore

To gaze upon her in her winter coat
Dressed in beads of ivory glow
Chilled to the bone
Smiling beneath the Christmas star
That meadow of our ripe imaginations
The midnight dream
Each seeing as the first time

Epilogue

This Book has been a long time coming. The words have been brewing since I could first hold a pen. The needed a lot of dusting off and seasoning. It's sometimes hard to put the private places out into the light. Part of me wants to keep them tucked away.

We all have our unwritten stories to tell. Ones we've lived. Ones we've moved through vicariously and those we dreamed of on our own. My father taught us the importance of passing on those treasured tales. Father to daughter, old man to young boy. Even when I don't take pen to paper they lay swimming around in my head. Fermenting and ripening. Then when properly cooked awakening(as my friend David would say).

It feels good to put them down. As if they can survive out there on their own no matter whether we are here or gone from this world. How I wish I'd written more of my Papa's stories down. You always hope your father and mother will be around forever (though the heart knows otherwise).

It seems I can bring him back by pouring through the remembered cadences and colorful expressions that were pure PK. Then it comes to me slowly. I don't carry all the endings and beginnings but I can see his smile. Hear his deep down in the reservoir laughter. He's back with me once again. Traveling through time. Then it seems the stories have lingered after all.

I hope other daughters and sons find a way to pass on their stories to all those who will listen. For if we lose the stories we lose everything. We have to remember this. Each string of experiences is unique. Every story has a life of its own.

When I write the stories I've been given I'm never quite sure where the words come from. I do know there's some spiritual intervention somewhere along the way and for that I'm grateful.

This collection of stories was a labor of love. Not everyone has been blessed with a Land to cherish. A place called Home. My sister said there's a high mountain lake where she always wanted her ashes buried. Though I have lived too many seasons away from my beloved Valley when I think of my last days I think of a resting place beneath those sweet White Mountains bathed in evening's pink light. A sign of God's mighty presence. I used to feel sorry for those folks who did not come from a magical place.

As I am writing this I am thinking of one of my last journeys to my homeland. Picturing morning out my Mother's window, the Sierras dusted with snow. I can hear the dogs barking at falling leaves and children playing. It is both a fresh memory and a sad reminder that I am too far away to walk the river, too distant to hear the rolling roar of afternoon thunder. One cannot live in two places at the same time but we can keep our heart spread between two open lands.

There are probably not enough words in the dictionary to paint this sacred valley properly. To tell of the places where my dreams were born. To capture the town that bears the hope and imaginings of all those who went before.

Sometimes it seems we shouldn't even try.

That one must see it for themselves. Perhaps these stories will get some folks on the roads due east in search of truth, home and the raw power of the Creator.

I can tell you this. If you can't find it here in the sacred Sierra Lands you won't find it anywhere.

Resource Information

Bishop Chamber of Commerce
www.bishopvisitor.com

Benton Area-Calif.
historicbentonhotsprings.com

Central Nevada Museum
cnmuseum@citlink.net
1900 Logan Field Road
Tonopah, Nevada 89049

Eastern California Museum
155 N. Grant St.
Independence, Calif 93526
Tel#760-878-0364
inyocounty.us/ecmsite

Keough's Hot Springs
Bishop, Calif. keoughshotsprings.com

Mizpah Hotel
100 Main St.
Tonopah, Nevada mizpahhotel.net

Mono County Museum/Historical Society
PO Box 417
Bridgeport, Calif 93517
Tel#760-932-5281 monocomuseum.org

Mammoth Museum

5489 Sherwin Creek Rd
Mammoth Lakes, Calif 93546
www.allmammoth.com/historymuseums
Tel#760-934-6918

Laws Railroad Museum

PO Box 363
Bishop, Calif 93515
www.lawsmuseum.org

Town of Tonopah

102 Burro Ave
Tonopah, Nevada 89049
Tel.775-482-6336

Tonopah Historic Mining Park

520 McCulloch Ave.
PO Box 965
Tonopah, Nevada 89049-0965
Tel#775-482-9274
TonopahHistoricMiningPark.com

Tom's Place

8180 Crowley Lake Dr
Crowley Lake, Calif.93546
Tel#760-935-4239
www.tomsplaceresort.com

About The Author

Butler is the author of three previous books and her work has been selected for a number of Anthology publications. She has worked as a free-lance writer for a number of years. Her work has appeared in magazine publications, newspapers and corporate publications.

Butler was awarded the Silver Pen Award from the San Jose Mercury News and honored by Embassy International in 2006.

Butler grew up in the Eastern Sierras of California and lived in the San Francisco Bay Area and the Napa Valley before moving to Palm Springs. Butler is currently working on a Play titled "Forgotten Women of The West" and finishing a Collection of Short Stories about her Travel Adventures. Butler is an artist, photographer and traveler when she is not writing short stories & poetry.

www.ingramcontent.com/pod-product-compliance
Lightning Source LLC
Chambersburg PA
CBHW020144180626
46810CB00004B/1722